CAMPUS EVANGELISM HANDBOOK

A Practical Guide for Showing & Sharing God's Love

Edited by **A**ndrés **T**apia

INTERVARSITY PRESS
DOWNERS GROVE, ILLINOIS 60515

© 1987 by **U** magazine.

All rights reserved. No part of this book may be reproduced in any form without written permission from InterVarsity Press, P.O. Box 1400, Downers Grove, Illinois 60515.

InterVarsity Press is the book-publishing division of InterVarsity Christian Fellowship, a student movement active on campus at hundreds of universities, colleges and schools of nursing. For information about local and regional activities, write Public Relations Dept., InterVarsity Christian Fellowship, 6400 Schroeder Rd., P.O. Box 7895, Madison, WI 53707-7895.

Distributed in Canada through InterVarsity Press, 860 Denison St., Unit 3, Markham, Ontario L3R 4H1, Canada.

Cover illustration: David Zentner

ISBN 0-8308-1213-X

Printed in the United States of America

Library of Congress Cataloging-in-Publication Data
The Campus evangelism handbook.

1. Evangelistic work.   2. College students—
Religious life. I. Tapia, Andrés, 1960-
BV3793.C36 1987   248'.5   87-31132
ISBN 0-8308-1213-X

17	16	15	14	13	12	11	10	9	8	7	6	5	4	3	2	1
99	98	97	96	95	94	93	92	91	90	89	88	87				

Preface

Christians are strange people. In many ways they are like everyone else—they struggle with anger, loneliness, difficult relationships, financial problems, falling grades, unemployment and so on.

But they are also very different. Why would they want to go out of their way and use their time and energy to talk to strangers about the abundant life that Jesus gives? We all have enough things to worry about, and we have enough friends and family members that need us without having to seek ways to also worry about the lives of people we don't even know.

The reason, of course, is Jesus Christ. He has touched us—despite all our blemishes—and told us he loves us. His love transforms us as he heals our hurts, gives us vision, shows us who we are. Our relationship with him is so real we find it hard to contain ourselves—we must talk about him. Not only that, but as we invite Jesus to make us more like him, his concerns, his pains, his longings become ours. Jesus is crying out to those who don't know him. And he has chosen (for whatever mysterious reason) to do a lot of it through us.

Now if the above paragraph does not ring true, then evangelism will always be a dreadful chore for you. In order to joyfully and freely share about the giver of life, you must experience him. If you're not, you need to take stock of your relationship with God. Does he feel far away? Do you wonder if he loves you? Many Christians *know* Jesus loves them but don't *feel* it. If this is the case for you, take the next several months to seek God in these areas—this is essential before you can really make sharing your faith a natural part of your life.

This leaves us with two important questions.

First, why evangelism? Sometimes even when we feel the joy and freedom of knowing Jesus, we still feel fear and guilt when it comes to sharing our faith with others. The thought of talking about something very close to our hearts with people who might be totally antagonistic toward it is not something we look forward to. Who wants to face rejection? And many of us have experienced the embarrassment of really blowing it for Christ. So why do we do it?

The answer is *love*. We love because God first loved us.

Only love can motivate you to reach out from inside yourself, to lay aside many of your dreams and goals, to give up your comforts and to touch those whom you don't know and who don't know Jesus. It is love that can drive out fear—fear of rejection when you share your message, fear of failure, fear of not knowing what you're doing. Guilt-free evangelism takes place as your security is rooted in Christ and not in what others think.

Second, what is evangelism? It is introducing people to the most wonderful friend around. This is the essence of the Christian faith—that you can have a relationship with *the God of the universe.* While he is Lord of your life, King of the cosmos and

Everlasting Father, he also is a God who became man and dwelt among us. No other religion espouses such an unlikely god.

This book arises out of the need to answer these questions. And not just in a theoretical/theological way, but in real and practical terms. Most of the answers to these questions are answered by the stories of people like you who have found exciting and healthy ways to share their faith.

To encourage you, each section opens up with an actual picture of evangelism taking place on campus. And the sections deal with a variety of issues:

☐ understanding your campus and how evangelism fits into your school's scene;

☐ getting a handle on what *is* the message after all and how people come to Jesus;

☐ presenting your faith to the different kinds of people in your life, such as friends, international students, Greeks, profs and family;

☐ understanding your faith intellectually;

☐ determining how your campus fellowship can have a lasting impact on campus.

In this book people share how they've talked about Jesus on campus. They tell their stories—their successes and their failures—in loving others for Jesus' sake. Talking about Jesus and seeing him change people's lives is addictive. If you implement even just a few of their many suggestions for how to make Jesus an issue in your friends' lives and on campus, you'll never be the same.

Andrés Tapia

What Do Non-Christians Think of Us?

Evangelistic Snapshot

One evening, *as we were reporting and sharing our concerns* in our small group, Susan requested prayer for her non-Christian sister who was seriously ill. Our questions to Susan unmasked a series of complex circumstances. Her sister's marriage had alienated her sister from the rest of her family. The couple was facing crippling medical expenses, and the pressures were threatening their shaky relationship. Beyond praying, we asked if we could help. Someone suggested we show our care by giving Susan money to pass on to her sister to help with hospital bills. We combined our resources to collect several hundred dollars.

At the next group session, Susan was in orbit. She had gone home and spent the weekend with her sister. She played back how she had given her our gift on Friday evening. Her sister had been staggered that people who did not know her and would probably never meet her, had given her money—especially since they were students!

The next morning, Susan's sister raised the matter of why her friends had been so generous. "People just don't do that kind of thing," was her charge. For the first time, Susan let her know that her friends were serious followers of Jesus. That revelation opened the door for a long discussion about God and what it meant to be a Christian.

Sunday morning Susan made her final hospital visit before returning to school for Monday's classes. Her sister greeted her with a smile and an announcement. "Well, I guess our family now has two Christians. I prayed for a long time last night, and I want to follow Jesus too."

While the rest of us were blinking back our tears, one member of our group exclaimed, "That's the best twenty bucks I've ever invested!"

—Don Posterski in *Why Am I Afraid to Tell You I'm a Christian?* (IVP).

Why I'm Not a Christian: A Report

by Robert Kachur

E*ffective campus evangelism requires directly addressing the ob*jections of unbelieving students and faculty. But what are these objections? If the good news is so good, why do most college students decide the gospel isn't for them?

The best way to answer these questions, the editors of U magazine decided, was simply to ask people. So we set out for three very different campuses: Northern Illinois University, a four-year state school; College of DuPage, a two-year commuter school; and Northwestern University, a private four-year "Big Ten" school. At each campus we set up a booth and offered students a free Coke (New, Classic, Diet or Cherry) if they would complete a brief, anonymous survey about religious faith, Christianity in particular.

Our goal wasn't to come away with statistics—we simply wanted students to tell us straight out how they perceive Christianity. Whether our perceptions are irrational, mistaken or right on, we all tend to base our decisions on them; we live as if our perceptions, right or wrong, tell the whole story. (For instance, a number of students said they shunned Christianity because of representative Christians like Jerry Falwell; Mother Teresa wasn't mentioned once.) If Christians desire to share their faith meaningfully, they must first ask, How do students perceive Christianity? How can we break through people's negative perceptions?

The results of our survey? Classic Coke whipped New Coke, with Cherry Coke coming in a close second. But more importantly, students identified several key factors that kept them from becoming Christians.

Hypocrisy

Q. Write the first thing that comes to mind when you hear the word Christianity.

A. People who don't practice what they preach.

The results at all three schools were unanimous: out of the eight options listed under "Why Christianity Does Not Appeal to Me," students chose "I've met too many Christians who are hypocritical and stuck-up" more than any other.

Often students whose other gripes against Christianity were very different saw eye to eye on hypocrisy; these people had either met lots of hypocrites, expected Christians to be perfect, or both. "The church is an escape valve for people to do things wrong and get told it was all right," one freshman wrote.

☐ *Sophomore chem major:* "Most Christians are hypocrites. If Christianity advocates giving to the poor, for example, why do Christians not give to the poor and instead defile the poor?"

☐ *Freshman business major:* A lot of Christians are just going along with the crowd; they say one thing with one group and something totally opposite with another."

☐ *Senior journalism major:* "Christians are supposed to care for each other—too often I see people stab each other in the back the moment they walk out of church."

☐ *Atheist sophomore:* "I used to be involved with my church, but as I got more and more involved, I found out what goes on in church and what goes on at home are two different things."

☐ *Junior journalism major:* "The thing about Christianity that bothers me is that many Christians are very narrow-minded people. Some aren't very nice. Jerry Falwell and other TV preachers use religion for their own benefit, and I think they prostitute the Bible. The Bible is a beautiful book from God—I hate to see it used to further specific political beliefs."

☐ *Senior chemistry major:* "The word *Christianity* makes me think of racism."

☐ *Freshman business major:* "Christianity's totally opposite of what it takes to survive on this planet. Christians are too self-oriented."

☐ *Junior film major:* "I'm not into religion at all—I tend to believe it causes wars."

Pride and Unacceptance
Q. Write the first thing that comes to mind when you hear someone say he or she is a "Christian."

A. Fundamentalist Protestants who pick apart your faith, no matter what you express it to be.

Perhaps the most devastating comments were students' descriptions of stuck-up Christians who enjoyed the brethren (and themselves) to the exclusion of other folk. To many non-Christians *Christianity* means "member of a big club," as one student put it. A significant number of students immediately thought of verbs like "look down on" and questionable adjectives like "elitist" and "well-dressed" when asked to describe the Christians they had met. And from the students we ran into, it seemed that when Christians weren't excluding others, they were being overbearing or insensitive. Some respondents, like one sophomore who labeled people who shared their faith "fanatics," were simply offended by evangelism of any kind. More objected to Christians who didn't seem to care about what non-Christians had to say.

☐ *Freshman data-processing major:* "Christians think they're too good for everyone else."

☐ *Senior English major:* "Christianity is a great idea, as is the idea of a benevolent power that people can gain reassurance from. However, I think that a religious belief which excludes people or encourages hatred based on personal belief is not something I want to participate in."

☐ *Freshman film major:* "Some Christians feel that they are glorified and anybody not in the group will go to hell, and this comes across as very pompous."

☐ *Freshman raised in a churchgoing home:* "Many Christians seem to think that anyone who does not exactly agree with them is a heathen who's not worth respecting."

☐ *Freshman journalism major:* "People tend to exclude others, whether they are Christian or not."

☐ *Music grad student:* "What bothers me most are Christians who push their views without caring about the other person's feelings, background, etc."

☐ *Nonpracticing Jewish history major:* "The worst is the way Christians look down on other religions and don't try to understand others."

☐ *Freshman, major undeclared:* "Follow what you believe, but listen to what others have to say—wrong or right."

Too Exclusive

Q. Why doesn't Christianity appeal to you?

A. I believe all religions are valid. God doesn't care how we worship as long as we are moral and love our neighbors.

We'd been standing in the rain at Northern Illinois for about an hour giving out wet Cokes when Joseph and his friend walked up to fill out surveys. As they leaned against a nearby wall to fill them out, Joseph began muttering. Finally he turned to us incredulously and blurted, "What do you mean 'Why doesn't Christianity appeal to me?' You can't jam your whole body into one way of thinking!" On paper he added: "There are too many people who see the world differently to limit yourself."

Joseph wasn't alone. Christianity's exclusivity proved to be the second most common reason students gave for not becoming Christians. Significantly, many who objected to Christianity's claim to be the only way to God seemed to associate Christianity's exclusivity with Christians who exclude or look down on others.

☐ *Buddhist journalism major:* "I don't like the way some Christians look down on other religions, especially Eastern philosophy. My religion is just as valid as theirs."

☐ *Senior political science major:* "I am Jewish. I am right in my beliefs. Someone else is Christian—they too are right! Why can't this seemingly illogical yet true statement just be accepted once and for all?!?"

☐ *Junior art history major:* "It seems that God would not exclude over half the world because they didn't accept Jesus."

☐ *Sophomore theater major:* "God's not so specific. Christianity is one of many plausible ways to a spiritual end."

☐ *Sophomore nutrition major:* "Any religion is good. You shouldn't be prejudiced about religion."

☐ *Psychology grad student:* "I know many Christians who are very intolerant of other beliefs—Protestants who don't like Catholics, Catholics who hate Jews, etc. There's one God and we all worship him in our own way."

☐ *Sophomore Asian studies major:* "Is Islam not also a religion worshiping the same God as Christians? There should be no sects."

☐ *Senior English major:* "Christianity's cool for others, but not my choice."

☐ *Freshman English major:* "You've got to be nuts to go through life believing that this is the only way."

At first students seemed to fall into three categories: Christians who believe Christ is the only way to God, non-Christians who believe there are many ways to God, and non-Christians who don't believe in or are indifferent to God. But a surprising number of those who checked "Christianity's too exclusive" also identified themselves as Christians who "try to apply the principles of (their) faith to everyday life." Interestingly, many of these folks had been going to church all their lives. How can students who seem to be committed Christians—like the practicing Roman Catholic of ten years who "enjoys talking to God"—also think Christianity's too exclusive?

Surveys, like people, can be tough to figure out. What's going through the mind of the sophomore who thinks both that "there's too much suffering in the world to believe in a loving God" and that people need Christianity because "the world's too tough to try and go it alone"? What about the theater major who doesn't know if she believes in God but sees herself remaining committed to the Protestant church for a long time? Or the two nursing students who'd been involved in the church for over fifteen years but checked "I don't really know much about Christianity"?

It's hard to say. People's perceptions stem from a variety of experiences. We don't always know how they fit together.

What Difference Will It Make?

So what did we learn from this exercise? First, that Christians need to ask themselves some hard questions about how they demonstrate their faith. For starters:

☐ Am I one of the hypocritical or stuck-up people these surveys referred to? Might others perceive me this way? What might be causing this perception?

☐ Is my church or fellowship group cliquish? Are friends and acquaintances who believe differently invited regularly? Would they feel comfortable if they came?

☐ How many friends do I have who believe differently from me or who profess no belief at all? (Wrote one Christian student: "Jesus spoke very strongly against snobbery and I want to change, but I still succumb to the 'holy huddle.' ")

☐ How much time during the average week do I spend with people who aren't Christians? Am I willing to accept the people around me and be a part of their world?

☐ When I tell others about my faith, do I have a hidden agenda of spiritual styles, petty cultural practices and political views that I assume the person must accept as part of the package?

☐ When I talk about matters of faith, do I click into a spiritual jargon that only other Christians can understand?

Christians should be prepared to live with labels such as "boring," "unsocial," "unable to think for themselves," "easily led" and "money-grabbing" until more of them are able to correct their shortcomings in the above areas. And even then it's easy to get discouraged—critics of the faith aren't always fair, and bad first impressions die hard. No matter what you do, some students will graduate and go to their graves saying what one junior told us: "It's my life."

Non-Christians, on the other hand, also need to be challenged about some of their more simplistic dismissals of the Christian faith. As well as demonstrating signs of authentic Christianity, we need to ask them,

☐ Are you willing to examine your simple beliefs about God and take a close look at how faith in God can affect your life? Do you resist Jesus because you know you'll have to change if you follow him? (Nearly all students we surveyed said they believed in God.)

☐ Does the fact that many Christians are hypocritical or stuck-up automatically mean that Christianity isn't true? (Or could it instead confirm the truth about Christianity that says all people without exception are sinners?)

☐ Are you willing to look past the cultural baggage many Christians carry around and examine the core of Christianity—that is, Christ?

When asked "What about Christianity appeals to you?" one student who couldn't think of anything wrote, "A free Coke appeals to me." We met a lot of thirsty students. But only Christians who care enough to get close to them—and thereby breaking the stereotypes—will have the chance to offer something infinitely more appealing than a free Coke.

I Saw Gooley Fly: A Parable

by Joseph Bayly

Herb Gooley was just an ordinary sort of guy until the night he stepped off his third-floor dorm window and flew away into the wild blue yonder.

But I'm getting ahead of my story.

I first met Gooley in that little hamburger joint just off the campus, Pete's Place. I'd never have noticed the guy except that he dropped a mustard jar and the stuff poured down his sport jacket. Now, I'm a sophomore at the time and this guy's a freshman. (No mistaking them during those early weeks of the quarter.) But he's making such a mess out of wiping the stuff off that I help him. Brother, that was really a mess. But Herb was the sort of guy who could hardly wipe his nose by himself—it wasn't just the mustard.

When we had the stuff pretty well wiped off his coat and shirt (you could still see these bright yellow streaks) I ask him where he lives.

"Pollard," he says.

"That hole. Must be a freshman, huh? You'll learn. 'Course, you can transfer after a quarter. Me, I'm at Sigma Phi House. Know that place that looks like a country club over on Lincoln?"

He doesn't know it. So we pay Pete and walk out. That is, I walk out. Herb trips over a cigarette machine that stands near the door.

Next time I notice the guy is at Homecoming.

It's during the freshman-sophomore tug of war. We're ready for the final pull and the gun goes off. I'll never know how he did it, but suddenly the whole freshman team's yelling to stop pulling. So we stop, and here's Gooley, looking sort of dazed, with the rope twisted clear around his arm. They get it off and take him to the health center. Nothing broken, but he sure must have had a painful arm for a few days.

I remember—sometime the following fall—seeing a crowd gathered around the front of Hinton's department store. So I pull over to the curb and here is the college van half in Hinton's show window. What a scene! Bodies all over the place, one of them broken in two across the hood. Gooley's standing there holding a head.

Maybe it was losing his driving privileges for a while got him interested in flying. At any rate he comes back from Christmas vacation his junior year able to fly. Able to fly, mind you, not able to fly a plane.

His roommate (Jerry Watson, it was) told us about it the next day. Seems Gooley had been studying late, and he finally turns the book over, switches off his desk light and says, "Think I'll go down to Pete's for a shake."

"Too late," Jerry says. "It's three minutes to twelve and he closes at midnight."

"I'll fly down." Gooley says it matter-of-factly, just like he's saying he'll run or something.

So over to the window he goes (Jerry all the while thinking Gooley is suddenly developing a sense of humor), lifts it up and steps off the ledge.

Their room is on the third floor.

Jerry waits a second for the thud, then dashes down the hall and down the stairs yelling, "Gooley fell out the window! Somebody call a doctor!"

No Gooley on the ground, or anywhere around. So they think Jerry's pulling their leg.

"Honest, guys, Gooley stepped out of our window. Said he'd fly down to Pete's. Honest he did."

So they wait around for Gooley to come back, and when he does they're all asking questions.

"Sure I can fly. Jerry was telling it to you straight. Here, I'll show you." And with that he takes off into the wild blue yonder.

None of us believed the story when we heard it. Would you? In the first place people can ride bicycles, people can row boats, people can fly planes even, but nobody can fly.

And if anybody could fly, Herb Gooley wasn't the man. That guy couldn't even walk.

It began to snow about supper time that day and snowed all through the night. Next morning the ground is covered and they've shoveled some walks off. I'm walking down the cleared path at the quad when I notice something. Fresh footprints go out on the snow a few yards; then there's nothing. Nothing. No feet turning around. Just feet going out there.

Within a few days nobody needs any more circumstantial evidence. We've all seen it. By it I mean Gooley flying.

He'd be walking along with you and suddenly he's airborne. Nothing spectacular. I mean it was all very quiet. His rise was almost vertical, and he flew along at about fifteen or twenty miles per hour. Just above the treetops. He'd sort of bank to turn.

That winter and spring you should have seen Gooley come into a class on the third or fourth floor of Old Main. Brother, that was a sight to behold. It got to be a regular custom to open the window just before the bell. I'll never forget the day we had a visiting lecturer. Nobody had told him.

Let me tell you there was a run on the library for books on aerodynamics, aircraft design and any other subject that even faintly bears on flying. Everyone was spending all their free time soaking up all they could learn.

I don't want you to get the idea that we talked a lot about it. Nobody would admit that they wanted to fly, but they all did. (Nothing in the world I wanted more. Seems sort of funny now.)

The college's flying course tripled in size. (Flying planes, that is, but it was as close as we could come to personal flight.) In the dorms we talked into the small hours about flying, speculating as to how Gooley did it.

You see, Gooley wasn't saying.

Of course later there was some reaction, when a lot of people began to call Gooley a freak. It sort of made us laugh though when one of the most outspoken anti-Gooleyites was found with a fractured skull at the foot of the Old Zach monument. (He got over it all right.)

I think the college administration was sort of ashamed of having Gooley as a student. So they bring in this guy Sikorsky for a special lecture series called "Flight Emphasis Week." Brother, were those lectures packed out—S.R.O.

Halfway through the week we realize that Sikorsky can't fly. We're standing outside Old Main, waiting for him to leave the president's office on the second floor. So how does he come down? Why, he takes the stairs down and comes out the front door. Sikorsky can design planes, he has the latest scoop on jets and helicopters, but he can't fly.

About a dozen students showed up for his final lecture.

Most of us had heard a myth about some ancient Greek who could fly until he got too near the sun. So we think maybe here's a clue. Interest switched to books on ancient Greek mythology, and the library places them on the reserve shelf.

You know, I've always been surprised that Gooley didn't tell us how to do it, or at least how he did it. He couldn't help knowing how interested we all were. But he kept his mouth shut. So none of us learned to fly.

It's a funny thing but I still have a sense of loss in not learning Gooley's secret. And other grads have confessed the same thing to me.

What happened to Gooley? I've often wondered about that. He transferred that fall to another college where, they say, all the students know how to fly.

What Is Evangelism?

Evangelistic Snapshot

Lois showed up at the evangelistic Bible study I had invited her to. As I began introducing the story of the woman at the well I suddenly remembered that Lois was living with her boyfriend, Phil, and that the passage dealt with a woman who had sexual problems. I feared Lois would think I had planned this just for her.

Thinking it would be better if Lois did not read the passage aloud, I called on Sally, who was immediately to my right, calculating that if each person read a paragraph aloud, we would finish before it was Lois's turn.

To my dismay a girl three seats away from Lois started reading. (I discovered later it was Sally's twin sister who had been sitting next to me.) Then Lois read the portion: "Jesus said to her, 'You're right in saying, "I have no husband" ... for the man you're living with is not your husband.' " It was her first experience reading Scripture and her eyes grew as big as saucers, while I hid behind my Bible!

"I must say, this is a bit more relevant than I had expected," she commented with considerable understatement. And as she saw with what sensitivity and perception Jesus interacted with the lonely woman, Lois's face showed how moved she was.

The next day Lois and I talked again. "Is there any reason why you couldn't become a Christian?" I asked.

"No," she said.

"Well, I can think of one," I said. "What will you do about Phil?" As we talked, tears and struggles were followed by an utterly sincere prayer asking Christ to come into her life as Lord.

After dinner that night I was talking with some students. Then we heard a noise and turned to see what it was. Here came Lois, slowly walking down the corridor, carrying several suitcases and smiling with tears streaming down her cheeks.

"I haven't left home," she replied to someone's query. "I've finally *found* my home. You see, today I became a Christian."
—Becky Pippert in *Out of the Saltshaker* (IVP).

What It Is and What It Isn't

by Terrell Smith

A friend of mine coaches a soccer team made up of six- to eight-year-old kids. During the new team's first two practices, he explained field positioning, the rules of the game, how to head the ball and the importance of passing. Halfway through the team's first game, he asked one of the players why he was letting the ball go by him all the time. "Oh," the little boy responded, "am I supposed to kick it?"

Often we get so caught up in the mechanics and strategies of doing something that we lose sight of the fundamentals. When it comes to evangelism—telling others about Christ—countless books have been published, seminars conducted, sermons preached. Somewhere along the line—often after several frustrated attempts—confusion, apathy and guilt set in, and soon we forget what evangelism is all about. Like the six-year-old soccer player, many of us have forgotten the basics.

Not only is knowing the basics of evangelism important, but it is also freeing. Let's look at what evangelism is *not* before we look at what it is.

What It Isn't

There are five things that evangelism is not. First of all, *evangelism is not defined by positive response.* The essence of our role in evangelism is not to make converts—that is God's work. It may be fair to ask whether our evangelism is biblical if we see no fruit, but our responsibility is simply to faithfully proclaim the message. God convicts and brings spiritually dead people into new life. You can't say, for example, that in Acts 17 Paul was not evangelizing because some mocked him and some didn't believe.

Second, *evangelism is not something we can turn on and off or schedule into our week.* Evangelism often becomes something we do at a particular time. Jesus said, "You are the light of the world," but we try to turn it on and off like a light bulb. Evangelism should take place in our day-to-day interactions. Planned evangelistic events are important, but those should take place in the context of having built strong relationships with non-Christians on your campus. Biblical evangelism is a lifestyle.

Third, *evangelism is not deceitful.* Many Christians (me included) have invited non-Christian friends to a Christian meeting where the gospel was going to be preached, conveniently forgetting to tell them about the evangelistic part. Once they're there, the gospel is dumped on them.

God does not need these little tricks. Instead, when we are honest and open, God will draw people to himself. Paul wanted to make sure he came clean: "For the appeal we make does not spring from error or impure motives, nor are we trying to trick you" (1 Thess 2:3).

Fourth, *evangelism is not distorted.* It's tempting to tamper with God's Word to make it more attractive, leaving out "little things" such as turning from and forsaking sin. To tell people that becoming a Christian means all your troubles will evaporate is also a lie. (If it is true, there were not any Christians in the New Testament.) Paul again: "We do not use deception, nor do we distort the word of God" (2 Cor 4:2).

I knew of a girl who believed that in order to present a clear picture of being a Christian she had to live a perfect, sparkling life before her roommate. She did it. She never let this roommate know that she had any problems or was struggling with anything. Her roommate eventually became a Christian and two weeks later committed suicide. She couldn't stand it. Her life still had problems which did not evaporate at conversion.

Fifth, *evangelism is not only for superevangelists.* Jesus did say, "Therefore go and make disciples of all nations . . . teaching them to obey everything I have commanded you" (Mt 28:19-20). But that doesn't mean we all have to become Billy Grahams. God has selected certain people in the church and given them gifts in evangelism, but he wants to use all his children in proclaiming his message. And he needs all types too. While it seems relatively easy for some extroverts to be aggressive in sharing their faith, their particular style may make it difficult for certain kinds of people to open up to them. Those people might be better ministered to by someone more shy and quiet.

Eloquence should not be a concern. Very often a shy person, an uneducated person or someone who just does not know how to say things with the right grammar or syntax can be very convincing because he speaks from his heart. Even though these people do not speak gracefully, they speak with such naturalness that everyone knows they are telling the truth.

What Evangelism Is

So what *is* evangelism? First, *it's the proclamation of a relationship,* rather than the proclamation of a doctrine or a list of dos and don'ts. The good news is that God forgives our sins because of Christ's death and resurrection, and that we can enter into a friendship with him. Therefore, communicating that Christians are learning to love God and building a relationship with him is vital to effective evangelism.

Second, *evangelism is done out of love rather than out of guilt.* As your relationship with God deepens, you will find yourself *wanting* to talk about him to others. How many have told themselves enthusiastically after hearing a dynamic speaker challenge the group about evangelism, "From now on, I'm going to be an excited evangelist. I'm going to go out and win the world." But within a few weeks all the zeal has seeped out—like an old, wrinkled helium balloon lying on the floor after being on the ceiling for a few days. Evangelism springs from the vitality of our relationship with God. No one suddenly says to herself, "I have decided that I am going to be excited about my fiancé." But many do exactly that with evangelism.

Evangelism is done not only out of love for God, but for other people. Of course, some people are less lovable than others. How do we learn to love the unlikable people, people who are annoying or who take up our time? One thing that always helps me are Jesus' words in Matthew 25 that when we serve the "least of these" we're also serving him. What a privilege! In addition, these "unlovables" end up teaching us a lot about love which we would never have imagined.

Third, *evangelism is hanging out with non-Christians.* Christians easily disengage themselves from much of non-Christian society. We dig our foxholes of fellowship so deep that we become like soldiers who have lost contact with the enemy. People have a need to be listened to, to be spoken to. Beneath the self-confidence and jokes lies a real person with emotional hurts and spiritual uncertainties. Someone who comes to people in openness, love and understanding is welcome.

Jesus said, "As the Father has sent me, I am sending you" (Jn 20:21). Jesus left his home in heaven to rub shoulders with promiscuous people and hedonists like us. Christians too have been sent by him. We need to leave our Christian ghettoes and rub shoulders with people.

Listen to people. When someone shares a problem, a curt

"I'll pray for you" sounds trite. Ask that person, "How can I help you in this?" Perhaps she needs prayer, but we also need to get involved in her life.

Fourth, *evangelism is communicating the message clearly.* It is great to know God and be where the people are. But something else is needed to do evangelism—a message. The facts about the person of Christ, his life, his death and his resurrection need to be told. People must know that they need to respond to these facts, by choosing to change their lifestyles and by placing confidence in the Lord.

Letting People Know

Plan to be used by God in evangelism. How? Pray, and in your prayers ask God for opportunities. Then expect God to open doors to good conversations.

With a little thought and prayer, witnessing situations can be created. In conversations with friends, ask questions like, "What are your goals in life?" instead of just, "How was your weekend?" There are many questions which can lead to a discussion about spiritual things. If people know you are a Christian, they'll be watching you and opportunities will open up.

Sometimes Christians think they can witness without saying anything. On a summer job I had when I was in college I decided I would witness silently. While the other guys were telling dirty jokes during lunch hour, I went off and read my Bible. As a consequence, I never had one significant conversation with anyone. I heard of another Christian student who used to play hymns on his fraternity's piano while his frat brothers were drinking at the bar. He never said anything. He just played and left, every night.

Paul asks (perhaps a bit sarcastically), "How, then, can they call on the one they have not believed in? And how can they believe in the one of whom they have not heard? And how can they hear without someone preaching to them? ... Consequently, faith comes from hearing the message, and the message is heard through the word of Christ" (Rom 10:14, 17).

As I was unpacking my books on the first day of my freshman year at college, I laid my Bible down on my desk. My new roommate saw it and said, "You're not some kind of a Christian, are you?" Actually he used words a little stronger than that. I was not sure how to answer because of the words he used. But just because I took my Bible out and laid it there, I was visible. And because he knew that I was a Christian, he watched me.

Amazingly, he talked to other guys. In my dorm there were two hundred guys. Guys I had never seen before would stop me and say, "Hey, I hear you're some kind of religious person. Tell me about it." My non-Christian roommate opened many doors for me just because of that Bible I unpacked.

God will open many more if you simply ask him.

Jesus' Style: Delightful and Disturbing

by Rebecca Manley Pippert

T*he essence of evangelism comes down to two things: the message is Jesus and the method is Jesus'*. Let's take a look.

Jesus came to us as the first whole person since Adam and Eve before the Fall. He is the model of what it means to be human. By following his lead we will not only become more like God himself but we will find ourselves becoming more comfortable with our humanity. And our evangelism will begin to flow naturally from who we are.

Jesus, One of Us

Jesus told us that as the Father sent him into the world, so he is sending us (Jn 17:18). How then did the Father send him? Essentially he became one of us. The Word became flesh (Jn 1:14). God didn't send a telegram or show evangelistic Bible study books from heaven or drop a million bumper stickers from the sky saying, "Smile, Jesus loves you." He sent a man, his Son, to communicate the message. His strategy hasn't changed. He still sends men and women—before he sends tracts and techniques—to change the world. You may think his strategy is risky, but that is God's problem, not yours.

In Jesus, then, we have our model for how to relate to the world, and it is a model of openness and identification. Jesus was a remarkably open man. He didn't think it was unspiritual for him (fully realizing he was the Son of God) to share his physical needs (Jn 4:7). He didn't fear losing his testimony by revealing to his disciples the depths of his emotional stress in the Garden of Gethsemane (Mk 14:32-52). Here is our model for genuine godliness. We see him asking for support and desiring others to minister to him. We must learn then to relate transparently and authentically to others because that is God's style of relating to us. Jesus commands us to go and then preach, not to preach and then leave. We are not to shout the gospel from a safe and respectable distance and remain uninvolved. We must open our lives enough to let people see that we too laugh and hurt and cry. If Jesus left all of heaven and glory to become one of us, shouldn't we at least be willing to leave our dorm room or Bible study circle to reach out to a friend?

There is also confusion about what it means to be spiritual. We feel it is more spiritual to take our non-Christian roommate to a Bible study or to church than to a play or out for pizza. Not only do we not understand our natural points of contact with the world: we don't understand our natural points of contact with God himself. He made us human. He is therefore interested in every aspect of our humanness. We dare not limit him to Bible studies and discussions with Christians. He created life and he desires to be glorified in the totality of life. And his power and presence will come crashing through to the world as we let him live fully in every aspect of our lives.

Jesus the Delightful
Once I reread the Gospels out of a desire to "rediscover Jesus."

In order to master the life of the Master, we need to grapple in radical, accurate and penetrating ways with the Gospels as they reveal the person of Jesus. As I read again, Jesus struck me with fresh force.

My first impression was that Jesus was utterly delightful. He enjoyed people. He liked to go to parties and to weddings. He was the kind of man people invited to dinner. And he came. He went to where they were. When two men first approached him, they became tongue-tied and unsure of what to say (Jn 1:35-39). When Jesus asked them what they wanted, they responded, "Oh, well . . . we were kind of wondering where your apartment is." Now Jesus knew that how he decorated his apartment was not the burning issue in their hearts. But instead of delivering a sermon, he took them *home* with him and they became his disciples. Later some of their relatives were among the first people he healed. But Jesus was more than merely charming; he cared about building a sense of family.

Jesus established intimacy with people quickly. Partly it was because he was open, but also because he understood people and wanted to establish rapport. He let people know that he had a sense of who they were and that he appreciated them. The first thing he did upon meeting Simon was to give him a nickname. The first thing he told Nathaniel was that he recognized the basic honesty of his character. Jesus drew people. Some came because Jesus recognized who they were, others because they had glimpsed something of who he was. His love was extravagant, almost reckless—never cautious or timid. He was approachable, he wanted people to know it, and they did.

The people of Jesus' day thought holy men were unapproachable. But Jesus' work was in the marketplace. He made people feel welcome, and that they had a place. His life was a constant demonstration that there were only two things that really mattered in this life—God and people. They were the only things that lasted forever. He was profoundly committed to setting people free and making them whole. He touched people at the deepest level. He wanted to heal not only blindness and leprosy, but the things that prevented joy and beauty, and freedom and justice.

Jesus was a compassionate man. He cared deeply and was not afraid to show it. The Stoics may have been proud of concealing their tears, but he never concealed his. He showed them plainly on his open face, whether he was weeping for a city or for a friend's loss. He healed people because he cared about them, not merely so they would follow him.

On one occasion a leper came to Jesus, no doubt full of shame and wounds (Mk 1:40-45). Desperate but timid, he said, "Well, if you want to, I think you could heal me." And Jesus, moved with compassion and looking at him steadily said, "Oh, I want to," and healed him.

I was also struck by the practical dimension of Jesus' compassion. His feelings were no deeper than his practical concern. He healed Jairus's daughter, and at the moment of a stupendous miracle, he simply told them to get her something to eat. His care was consistent. Never flashy, sometimes almost quiet. Even after his death, Jesus demonstrated the very same care. If I had resurrected, I think I would have rented the Coliseum and staged the Mormon Tabernacle Choir to sing the "Hallelujah Chorus." But in one postresurrection account (Jn 21) we find Jesus making the disciples a little breakfast!

Jesus was a sensitive man. He had an extraordinary ability to see what people longed for, or really believed, but were afraid to reveal. To the leper in Mark 1:40-45 he could have shouted, "Be healed . . . but don't get too close. I just hate the sight of lepers." He did not. Jesus reached over and touched him. Jesus' touch was not necessary for his physical healing. It was critical for his emotional healing.

Can you imagine what it meant to that man to be touched? A leper was an outcast, quite accustomed to walking down a street and seeing people scatter and shriek at him, "Unclean—unclean!" Jesus knew that this man not only had a diseased body but an equally diseased self-concept. He needed to be touched as well as cured. And so Jesus responded as he always did, with total healing for the whole person.

Jesus was a passionate man. If someone had asked me as an agnostic several years ago to describe what I thought Jesus was like, I would have readily given an answer. I pictured him as a sweet, kind man, his hair parted down the middle with a kind of "Halo shampoo" effect. I thought he probably spent most of his time skipping along the shores of Galilee, humming religious tunes with his disciples—the kind of person everyone would love, especially your mother. I sincerely believed this and did not think it was the least irreverent. Granted, the depth of my biblical understanding stemmed largely from Cecil B. De-Mille—and Hollywood seems to have a knack for making spirituality and severe anemia almost synonymous. But even from the few Christians I knew, I sensed that Jesus was wimpy.

Then one day I looked at the New Testament. Instead of the meek, mild man I had always assumed Jesus to be, I found a man of profound passion. An extraordinary being, flinging furniture down the front steps of the temple, casting out demons and asking people how they expected to escape the damnation of hell. He said such weak innocuous things as, "I came to cast fire upon the earth" (Lk 12:49). The thing I quickly perceived after seeing this shattering personality which fills the Gospels is that having once gotten even a glimpse of him, I could never again say, "Oh, how interesting."

Jesus the Exasperating

If my first impression of Jesus was that he was delightful, another equally forceful impression was that he was exasperating. Wherever he went he produced a crisis. He compelled individuals to decide, to make a choice. In fact he struck me as the most crisis-producing individual I had ever encountered. Eventually nearly everyone clashed with Jesus, whether they loved him or hated him.

A friend of mine has said that he always discovered a lot about a person when he knew who liked the person and who did not. In Jesus' case, we have the story of the holiest man who ever lived and yet it was the prostitutes and lepers and thieves who adored him and the religious who hated his guts.

What do you do with a man who is supposed to be the holiest man who has ever lived and yet goes around hugging prostitutes and lepers? What do you do with a man who not only mingles with the most unsavory people but actually seems to enjoy them? The religious accused him of being a drunkard, being a glutton and having tacky taste in friends. As my friend Gene Thomas is fond of saying, "Jesus was simply not your ideal Rotarian." It is a profound irony that the Son of God visited this planet and one of the chief complaints against him was that he was not religious enough.

The religious of his day were offended because he did not follow their rules and traditions. He was bold and outspoken. He favored extreme change and valued what they felt was insignificant, which was largely the "unlovely."

What did he say to them? Well, I think Jesus would have been my *last* choice as a speaker for a fund-raising drive. To say he was not the master of subtlety would be putting it mildly. Imagine a scene in which you would gather all the powerful and religious elite so they could hear Jesus give a talk. (Mt 23 describes such a scene.) They are seated, Jesus comes out and his opening words are "You bunch of snakes. You smell bad. You kind of remind me of decomposed bodies walking around. You're hypocrites and blind guides. And I want to thank you very much for coming." It was not exactly a speech that endeared them to Jesus.

But for those who loved him he was equally exasperating. He constantly kept smashing some of his followers' expectations of what the Messiah should do. He simply did not fit their mold. He did not try to. They thought the Messiah would come in power and liberate Jerusalem, in their Maccabean tradition. But the only power that Jesus demonstrated was the power of servanthood. His disciples wanted to know who would be first in terms of prestige. Jesus told them the first would be the greatest servant. For Jesus' greatness was seen not in the degree to which he was elevated, but the degree to which he came down and identified.

Jesus was a confident man. He was secure and he knew who he was. While other religious leaders were often self-effacing, Jesus was self-advancing. Other religious leaders often required their followers to obey rules or laws or "a way." Jesus said, "I'm the way and the truth and the life" (Jn 14:6). Based on that, we are asked simply to follow him. Jesus didn't make suggestions, he uttered commands ("come to me," "follow me," "drop your nets").

I think we can safely say that Jesus was hardly the victim of a poor self-concept. He was the Son of God. All these traits—his delightfulness, his compassion, his sensitivity, his passion, his ability to establish rapport as well as to exasperate—all sprang from the fundamental fact of his deity.

But the continuing question that Jesus faced because of his claims and actions was voiced the loudest by the Pharisees. They saw Jesus healing on the Sabbath and asked, "Who do you think you are, healing on the Sabbath?!" And Jesus answered, "The Lord of the Sabbath." There were no more questions.

Which leads me to my last impression of this towering figure. How did Jesus justify his behavior which seemed to eventually lead everyone into conflict or crisis? I think it could be stated briefly like this: "I do what I do, because I am the Lord—and you are not. You follow me. I do not follow you." His answers were most often that simple. He said he was the Lord. He knew it. He lived like it. He acted like it. And he wanted people to respond accordingly.

Changing the World

How can we relate to people in a way that will change the

world? Jesus loved and changed the world in two ways: by his radical identification with men and women, and by his radical difference. Jesus seemed to respond to people by noticing first what they had in common (Jn 4:7). But it was often in the context of their similarities that Jesus' difference came crashing through (Jn 4:10).

It was as people discovered Jesus' profound humanness that they began to recognize his deity. God's holiness became shattering and penetrating as Jesus confronted people on their very own level of humanity. But the point is that it took both, his radical identification and his radical difference, to change the world. So it will be for us.

Four Roads to Faith

by Samuel Escobar

How *do people come to Jesus and enter into a relationship* with him? What paths do most people travel to find Christ?

We usually think people become Christians by hearing the message, following steps 1, 2, 3, 4 and coming to a decision. But this presupposition is too narrow—and so is our evangelism if we follow it.

Ask some people in your church or fellowship how they became Christians, especially those who do not come from a church background. You'll be surprised with the circumstances and ways of their conversions. I have done it, and my conclusion is that there are at least four different avenues to Christ: through the search for truth, interest in a person, the challenge of commitment and the touch of power. We need to know how to meet a friend's need at any of these four levels.

The Search for Truth

The search for truth is the most common road to faith, the one to which we refer most when we think about evangelism.

We have a biblical example in the Gospel of John. This man, Nicodemus, comes to Jesus with questions. The way Jesus speaks to him is instructive.

> There was one of the Pharisees named Nicodemus, a member of the Jewish Council, who came to Jesus by night. "Rabbi," he said, "we know that you are a teacher sent by God; no one could perform these signs of yours unless God were with him."
>
> Jesus answered, "In truth, in very truth I tell you, unless a man has been born over again he cannot see the kingdom of God."
>
> "But how is it possible," said Nicodemus, "for a man to be born when he is old? Can he enter his mother's womb a second time and be born?" (Jn 3:1-4 NEB)

So this man is serious enough to come with his questions and concerns. He comes to Jesus because he sees in Jesus a rabbi, a teacher. He comes in search of teaching. He wants to be taught; he wants to know. He has some questions; he pursues these questions, and Jesus answers him.

In colleges today many people come to Christ that way. Some kind of intellectual curiosity brings them to their first contact with a Christian group. They have some questions; they are asking; they are searching. Maybe theirs is not an elaborate philosophical search, but it is still a search for truth.

I was talking with a group of students in Calgary, Canada, who were telling how they became Christians. One of them said, "Well, I saw an ad about a discussion the Christian club was having on witchcraft and Christianity. I was interested in the whole issue of witchcraft. The ad caught my attention and I went to the discussion because I had some questions."

That's the way he became a Christian. There are some in your group who came because of an idea on a poster that attracted them. They were interested in the idea and wanted to pursue it. Like Nicodemus, they came because something piqued their curiosity; they had questions.

Interest in a Person

In the Gospel of Luke we meet someone whose interest in a person brought him to faith: "Entering Jericho [Jesus] made his way through the city. There was a man there named Zacchaeus; he was superintendent of taxes and very rich. He was eager to see what Jesus looked like" (Lk 19:1-3 NEB).

For Zacchaeus, unlike Nicodemus, it is not so much a question of ideas. It is more an interest in people, a person—"I want to see what he looks like!"

"But, being a little man, he could not see him for the crowd. So he ran on ahead and climbed a sycomore-tree in order to see him, for he was to pass that way. When Jesus came to the place, he looked up and said, 'Zacchaeus, be quick and come down; I must come and stay with you today.' He climbed down as fast as he could and welcomed him gladly" (Lk 19:3-6 NEB).

There is no intellectual exercise at all, no questions answered, no search for truth. This is a personal encounter, a relationship. This man wants to know what Jesus looks like.

He probably is a solitary man (tax collectors were not popular). What is his need? His need is for a meaningful relationship. That's where it itches! And so what is Jesus' answer? He says, "I'm going to stay in your home and eat with you." In that Eastern situation, nothing could be more expressive of Jesus' desire to take him seriously as a person and to risk having his friendship.

Jesus was called a friend of publicans and sinners. For some, truth is in people and they want to have a meaningful relationship with others that will really get them to the truth.

The Challenge of Commitment

Perhaps the Bible's most interesting example of this road to faith is Paul, who here in Acts 9:1-6 is called Saul:

Meanwhile Saul was still breathing murderous threats

against the disciples of the Lord. He went to the High Priest and applied for letters to the synagogues at Damascus authorizing him to arrest anyone he found, men or women, who followed the new way, and bring them to Jerusalem.

While he was still on the road and nearing Damascus, suddenly a light flashed from the sky all around him. He fell to the ground and heard a voice saying, "Saul, Saul, why do you persecute me?"

"Tell me, Lord," he said, "who you are."

The voice answered, "I am Jesus, whom you are persecuting. But get up and go into the city, and you will be told what you have to do." (NEB)

Saul's life can be described in one word: commitment. He is a committed man. He is a go-getter, an avowed anti-Christian. He is entirely immersed in the cause of Judaism. He sees the Christians as a danger. And probably the only thing that will take him out of one type of commitment will be something that is worth more than what he is committed to now.

The stoning of Stephen may be a key in all this. It's a moving scene. Stephen is just a layman, not one of the apostles, but he is a strong man who gives a brave and powerful message: "How stubborn you are, heathen still at heart and deaf to the truth! You always fight against the Holy Spirit. Like fathers, like sons. Was there ever a prophet whom your fathers did not persecute?" (Acts 7:51-52 NEB).

Stephen's words so infuriated the crowd that the people dragged him out of the city and stoned him. And Saul was among those who approved of Stephen's murder.

It was there that God started to speak to Saul. He saw that Stephen was a committed man who died for his cause. The one who is committed is impressed by the commitment of others. That's the only thing that can challenge him or her. So the next mention of Paul in Acts is his conversion in Acts 9. And Paul's commitment to Jesus has the same fervency he had when he was persecuting the followers of his new Lord.

The lack of commitment of many Christians is why it's difficult to communicate the gospel to very committed people—for example, Marxists. You can only change committed people by showing more commitment. The way they see it, if God is God, he demands more, and he is worth not only living for, but also dying for.

That's why I became a Christian—because I wanted the same kind of commitment my Marxist friends had.

Marxism didn't attract me intellectually. I had gone through a course on Christian apologetics in high school, and my mind was sharpened in the process of trying to answer spiritual questions. But I was put to shame by the *commitment* of my Marxist friends.

After trying for months and months, I finally got my friend Hector to my church. Hector is a Marxist who later became the leader of the guerillas in Peru. It was Saturday, the day of a social meeting for young people.

At the end of the evening, I was talking with him and I said, "Tell me, Hector, what do you think about our church?"

And he said, "Well, you know, it's very easy to be a Christian."

"What do you mean?"

"They give you a room, they give you a Ping-Pong table, they give you hot chocolate after the meeting. You have a great time there. Do you know that I am risking my life for the party? They don't give me anything! Do you know that I have to give so many hours of my time a week to do this and that for the party? It's too easy to be a Christian."

That kind of shocking experience made me take my Christianity seriously. Some people come to Christ only when they are challenged by a commitment greater than their own.

The Touch of Power

There is one more avenue to Jesus which we see over and over in Scripture—namely, through the touch of his power. We have an example of it in the Gospel of John:

[In Bethesda] lay a crowd of sick people, blind, lame, and paralysed. Among them was a man who had been crippled for thirty-eight years. When Jesus saw him lying there and was aware that he had been ill a long time, he asked him, "Do you want to recover?"

"Sir," he replied, "I have no one to put me in the pool when the water is disturbed, but while I am moving, someone else is in the pool before me."

Jesus answered, "Rise to your feet, take up your bed and walk." The man recovered instantly, took up his stretcher, and began to walk. (5:3-9 NEB)

Now this man comes to Jesus in a different way, by a different route: by feeling Jesus' touch of power. And many these days come to him that way.

Don't misunderstand me; many people whom Jesus healed didn't even come back to say thank you. Do you remember the ten lepers? Nine of them went away without even saying thanks. A miracle was no guarantee that people would become followers of Jesus. He didn't use miracles for that.

What I am saying is that Jesus comes to the lives of some people not after an intellectual search nor by some of the other roads that we have mentioned, but rather through his own act of power in their lives.

While traveling in the Maritimes of Canada, I saw former drug addicts who had come to Christ because Christ had been powerful in their lives in a way no one could explain. Nothing else had been able to get them off drugs—no doctors, no psychologists, no social workers, no police. But simply a powerful act of God shocked them, got them off of drugs and helped them at a crucial moment in their lives. No intellectual argument, nothing else. Just a powerful act of God.

The Right Message for the Road
Now it is important to consider how we, as individuals and as a group of Christians, can help the people in each of these four

categories. What kind of evangelism will reach each of them and help them find fullness of life in Christ?

People on a *search for truth* need to be taken seriously. If you take time to listen to their questions and to point them to answers in the Scripture or to find answers for them when their questions are beyond you, they will appreciate your help.

If you give them a canned answer or simply tell them your own personal opinion on some issue, it will lack authority and they may disdain it. Be careful not to treat their questions with scorn. You may think they are ridiculously simple, too complex to have any value or totally beside the point. But for them they are a valid part of the search for truth.

Also encourage them to talk to God directly about their questions—even if it means starting with "Do you exist?"

Provide books, offer to study Scripture with them, invite them to a good lecture or discussion of a Christian topic.

Respect their intellectual struggle. Above all, support the facts you give with an attitude of caring which can represent Christ to them. All of us need both truth and love. The next chapter, "The Search for Truth" by Rich Lang, will help you understand these people.

For the curious *who want to encounter something in a person,* you may be the one they need to see as a "friend of sinners" before they are willing to approach the Lord Jesus Christ. What they see in you day by day is what they consider the Christian message to be—for, after all, you are a Christian.

The best thing you can offer this kind of person is to share your life with him or her, honestly and openly. Let your friends see your struggles as well as your victories. Admit your problems and needs. Let them watch as you pray—and as God answers. Include them in Bible studies if they are willing. Try to have them get to know other Christians so this meaningful relationship will not be just with you but with the family of God. Make it clear that the real heart of Christianity is a personal relationship with God himself. "Meeting Jesus through Friendships," by

Paul Tokunaga, exemplifies this path to Christ.

To the *committed person* (no matter to what cause he or she is presently committed), your own commitment will be a key in witness. If you are not taking your discipleship to Christ very seriously, you have nothing to say to this person.

Actually, the people who want a cause to give themselves to are better candidates for Christian conversion than the merely curious or the ones who want a cure-all for their problems. We must never misrepresent the gospel by pretending it is easy to answer Christ's call; we must include the fact that he says "take up your cross daily and follow me."

As our committed friends see us doing this, not seeking the comfortable way all the time, they will at least respect our gospel and may become willing to study Scripture with us on a regular basis. Consider using Ada Lum's study guide *Jesus the Life Changer* (IVP). You may also be able to include them in a social action project you are involved in. Melissa Moskowitz may give you insights into these people in "Attracted to Commitment."

We all need *the powerful acts of God* in our lives. Watch for God's workings both in your own life and in theirs as you dare to pray for the power of God to make itself manifest in your midst. Praying *with* and not just for your friends and their needs is a step of faith that can create wonderful opportunities to see God in action. Rob Decker, in "Encounter with Power," explains how wonderful the opportunities can be.

Keep in mind a few correctives: for those who are looking too much for something that will make them "feel good," help them get some facts as a basis for their faith; for those who have come to Christ through the intellectual route, point them toward the reality of a dynamic relationship with the living Christ; for those who have come out of the attraction of the commitment, caution them about falling into performance orientation—wanting to do things for Christ to get his approval; and finally, for those who came to Christ through God's manifestation of power, help them to remember that good friendships are still the most powerful way in which people experience Christ.

Above all, remember that evangelism is simply the sharing—and demonstration—of the gospel. It is God, not us, who saves. Be fervent in prayer for a friend who needs Christ. Then, no matter by which avenue the person may come, the Lord is the one who can reach down, meet the needs, and bring him or her to a living faith. Nothing is too hard for our God.

The Search for Truth

by Rich Lang

I had not grown up believing in God. Not being raised in a particularly religious home, I came to view God as a quaint and sentimental myth for the false comfort of the ignorant and weak. I saw religion as a placebo for gullible children and frightened old people. So I tucked God away in the closet with Santa Claus and the Easter Bunny.

But a difficult childhood raised questions for me that would eventually lead along a path in search of God. When I was four years old my parents divorced. For several years my grandparents and relatives took care of my younger brother and me while my mom worked late hours to feed us. At times we felt abandoned, and I remember running away on occasion.

During my first few years in school, I felt insecure and distracted, and my grades told the same story.

When I was seven years old, my mom remarried. Alcoholism, more parental quarreling and child abuse plagued our family. We moved frequently. When I was ten, my mom again divorced and suffered a mental breakdown. Concerned relatives placed her in a state psychiatric institution where she remained for ten years.

My brother and I then went to live with our father and step-mother. This new setting was more healthy and stable, but the adjustments were still difficult.

In my new school and community I began to do well both socially and academically. My grades shot up, and I made many good friends. I got involved in gymnastics and the a cappella choir. Life was definitely looking brighter. Outwardly I seemed cheerful, friendly and involved. But inwardly I began to be aware of a deep detachment, loneliness and resentment. I couldn't say why, but I knew that for me life just did not add up. I could not make any real sense of it.

I wondered what kind of a world I was living in. I wondered what was truly worthwhile. I could see myself and others chasing after popularity, security, grades and good times. Yet somehow these all seemed shallow and empty to me.

Life seemed paradoxical. There was beauty and ugliness, wealth and poverty, friendship and alienation, pleasure and pain, health and sickness, justice and brutality, wisdom and stupidity, birth and death. What did it all mean? How could anyone know? It occurred to me that maybe we were all here by some terrible and cruel twist of fate. I could pretend that life had some meaning in the short run. But I could find no point in it in the long run. I asked myself, Does it even matter whether I live or die? What will come of what I do today or tomorrow? What will come of my whole life? Is there any meaning in my life that the inevitable death awaiting me will not destroy? I could not answer these questions. And yet a voice inside persistently cried out, "There must be something more!"

I do not remember when, but gradually I began to wonder if perhaps that "something more" might be God.

I could not know the answer, but I could see that if a good and benevolent God did exist, only then could life make sense.

Only then could my life have any ultimate value and meaning that would not be reversed by death. It was only a hypothesis, you understand, but it began to look like a necessary one if life were not to be reduced to an irrational jungle, to the red-in-tooth-and-claw struggle of the survival of the fittest. The question of God's existence here ceased to be a merely academic one. It suddenly took on life-or-death significance. Was I prepared to live consistently with the terrible implications of honest atheism? The "cheerful atheism" of some of my friends began to look utterly absurd and self-deluding to me. Could there be something more? I wondered.

Glimpses of God

During this time I became keenly interested in science, and especially astronomy, my surrogate religion. I obtained a telescope and spent many wonder-filled evenings peering out into the heavens, reveling in the vastness, beauty and haunting mystery of the universe.

The sense of wonder and exultation I so often felt did something to me. I often gazed into the inky sky and muttered under my breath, "Who are you? What Power or Presence is this that brings me into existence only to kill me? Will I ever find out why I have lived before I die? Please, if you are really there, show yourself to me."

I began to see more and more cracks in my atheism. Could I really believe that this extraordinarily complex and beautiful cosmos evolved mindlessly by chance?

How far this miracle of *homo sapiens* seemed from the dumb and instinctual grunts of apes in caves, much less the amoeba and protozoan. After all, I observed, we humans write books and tell stories; we paint pictures and compose symphonies; we love and marry each other; we study law and appeal to conscience; we fight for just causes and we die for freedom; we think about God and contemplate our destiny. Did all this come about by chance and does it count for nothing? To believe that the irrational and immanent forces of nature had created all this required too much faith for me! There had to be something more.

So it was that a dim and abstract hunch about the reality of God started to dawn upon me. I was still a long way from a positive and convinced belief in God. In school I was making the acquaintance of many Christians. Many of these people deeply impressed me. Their aggressive confidence in God and his activity in their lives disturbed me, but their earnestness and concern for people attracted me. I could see integrity, joy and hope in their faces. I was curious and desired to know from what source this inner confidence came. They seemed to know God with an intimacy and assurance I lacked.

Stan, especially, was helpful to me. He was a robust athlete, an honest and good-natured guy, a committed Christian and a good friend to me. As we studied, worked out and played together, Stan shared his faith in Jesus Christ. Highly skeptical, I regularly taunted him with sacrilegious jokes which he patiently endured. One day when conversation about God had reached an impasse, Stan looked me in the eye and said, "Rich, you'll never understand what I'm talking about until you realize that Jesus Christ is not a religion but a relationship. You have to realize who Jesus Christ is, and what he's done for us. Read the New Testament, and check it out for yourself."

Drawn to God

I hesitantly agreed and started to read the New Testament. I was not prepared for what began to happen as I read through its pages. I was arrested by the personality and authority of Jesus. His teaching and his miracles astonished me. Most of all I was struck by his personal claims. Here was a man who claimed to be the unique Son of the most high God. His enemies finally executed him for the crimes of blasphemy and treason, for he, being a man, dared to make himself equal with God and declared himself the sovereign ruler of an eternal kingdom, the kingdom of God. How could this be? This good, wise and miraculously powerful man dared to proclaim himself as the true Savior and judge of all men! *Incredible,* I thought.

What was I to think of Jesus? Here was one who claimed to forgive sins. Here was a man who healed the sick, cleansed lepers, cast out demons and raised the dead. Before me was a man who lived as never a man has lived, and who spoke as never a man has spoken. This man lived a perfect life. Even his enemies could not find fault in him. This man lived with love for his enemies. He said he was sent from the Father to give his life as a ransom for many, and to call us out of darkness into the eternal kingdom of God.

What was I to do with Jesus Christ? Could this be the one for whom my heart had waited? Was he a counterfeit or the Christ of God? For months I read and talked to others, believers and unbelievers. I weighed the question long and hard in my soul.

What would I decide about this friend to the socially forgotten and morally fallen? Was he a liar, this man of consummate moral integrity? It seemed unlikely. Was he a madman, this wise man of stunning insights? It seemed doubtful. Then was he a deliberate hoax of his disciples' invention? It would have taken a true genius to pull off such a story if it were not true. Why would his disciples be willing to die for what they knew to be fraud? The whole story had a ring of truth that struck me as self-evidently trustworthy. It appeared as if the great miracle had actually happened! What was I to do?

Meeting God

I stood at a spiritual crossroads. My quest began to shift from intellectual inquiry to personal moral confrontation. The more I looked at the perfect life of Jesus Christ, the more painfully aware I became of my own moral imperfections. What did I see in his face? Wrath? mercy? or was it both a fierce opposition to evil *and* a passionate love for those who desire to turn from their sin? As I pictured Jesus Christ hanging in agony upon that

Roman cross, the mind-reeling and heart-wrenching thought rushed over me, "Oh, God, he died for me! He is where I should be, taking my judgment! Somehow, he was the ransom!"

My eyes flooded with tears of joy in that sudden realization of my destitution and of God's love. I could feel the tears washing away years of fear, emptiness and guilt. Opening my heart and mind to the love of God in Jesus Christ was like no other experience in my life. I felt cleansed, like a new person inside. I publicly confessed my faith and was baptized.

Over the next months and years my parents and friends have recognized and told me that they have seen God make a profoundly positive and lasting difference in my life. Again and again God has proven himself to me. He has healed the memories and hurts of my past and given me the freedom of spirit to move on into a joyous and open future.

God has given me an abundant life. It is not a life without problems and difficulties, but it is a life with limitless divine resources. He has given me a clear calling, purpose in life and confident hope for eternity. In my search for truth I found answers—I found him.

Meeting Jesus through Friendships

by Paul Tokunaga

M*y relationship with Gary had a painful beginning. We* were players on opposite eighth-grade football teams. You don't easily forget a face that runs by you for touchdown after touchdown.

The next year as a high-school freshman in geometry I saw that smiling face again (as usual, I mostly saw the back of his head), this time in the seat in front of me. Thus began one of the most significant relationships of my short life (which is very nice when you're going through what seems to be the most insignificant class of your life). That year Gary became my friend, and in the turbulent, rocky and unpredictable years to follow, he stayed my friend.

The Hound of Heaven

Very little changed in my life that year, or even during my sophomore and junior years. But I did do some serious thinking about Gary's lifestyle and mine, both of which I watched closely. While my life conformed to the patterns of this world, his tended to work against many of those patterns.

The difference boiled down to this: My activities generally seemed to drag either myself or others down; Gary represented the only force on the horizon involved in pushing people upward and building positive character traits into their lives. He was unusual, and I saw it plainly.

Nonetheless, dynamic mediocrity prevailed. Life at home was miserable as I caused my family many hardships with a cruel attitude, a quick tongue and a fiery temper. The excitement of brushes with the law was never very satisfying. Some of my relationships with girls were not exactly satisfying either. "Cruising chicks" with the boys on Saturday nights seldom cut through the superficiality. Francis Thompson in *The Hound of Heaven* accurately describes my earlier years:

I fled Him, down the nights and down the days;

I fled Him, down the arches of the years;

I fled Him down the labyrinthine ways

Of my own mind; and in the midst of tears

I hid from Him, and under running laughter.

I knew there was a God. I occasionally tuned in on "Davey and Goliath" on Sunday mornings. I once won a plastic cross at the ring-toss booth at the local carnival (I was aiming for the pocketknife). Someone handed me a David Wilkerson tract at the beach when I was twelve (one of the greatest hit-and-run jobs I've ever witnessed). I once read a book on mealtime prayers when I was invited to eat dinner with a Catholic friend's family and was afraid I would be asked to say the blessing.

But most of all, I knew there was a God because I knew Gary. In a real sense, the Word became flesh and dwelt among me. No, Gary was not Jesus, but his life demonstrated the same kind of appealing consistency that Jesus' did. The good news of the gospel was etched deeply into his head and heart. As we spent time together—on the student council, playing basketball, he helping me with geometry problems—the stark contrast between the godly and the godless became evident.

Not that my life wasn't consistent in its own way. I was hurting—I knew it, and during the more honest and groping times, I would communicate it.

I remember some words I wrote in an essay for senior English. I called it "Spaces to Fill"; it was aimed at somebody, anybody who might fill them:

"Okay, I admit it. I am insecure. I am immature. I am a great waste to the world. But will you help me? Will you get me out of this mess? I need you to help me get out of the dark. Will you be the one to shine the light on *me*?"

God must have been listening. Two months after that essay was written he brought people—a small, loving, praying group of them—into my life to help me find my way to Jesus Christ.

Getting on the Roller Coaster

So began my life as a Christian. It was tremendously exciting and exhilarating. God was indeed real. "Believe in him!" I'd urge my pagan friends Jim and Tony, because I knew he answered prayer. Mom and Dad must have seen the difference in my life too—my New Testament was now getting equal time as posthomework reading along with Hugh Hefner.

Bliss. What better word could describe those first two weeks?

And what better word to describe the next two years than . . . *roller coaster?*

Jesus continually taught his followers that the secret to the kingdom of God is to hear the word of the King and act on it. "Consistent in the hearing and incredibly sporadic in the doing" aptly described my first few years as a Christian.

Tolerating sin, acting as stubborn as an ox, praying for one thing but doing another—these were traits characterizing my Christian life. But, thankfully, Gary responded to God's asking him to be a Paul to this young Timothy. And so God's kingdom slowly became a place in which I felt more comfortable living.

Now Gary was never a saint, never without blemish. Like me,

vice work, but we are truly brothers in Christ.

coming a Gary

no did God use to interest you in Jesus? What was it about at person that held your interest? Was there someone who ck it out with you during those lean times when God seemed ent and distant? Someone who didn't run away from you after e or she saw the "ugly things" of your life?

Was there a Gary in your life?

One of the most moving passages of the New Testament is und in John 21 where Jesus asks three times, "Do you love e, Peter?" When Peter says yes, Jesus tells him, "Feed my heep." I've wept over this passage several times because the mplications strike home all too deeply. I know how Jesus fed is sheep. He took risks socially, economically and politically or them. It cost him plenty.

Do you love Jesus? Are you willing to put aside that important and even crucial term paper when a dorm mate pounds on your door and asks for help?

Do you love Jesus? Will you patiently listen to a friend who wakes you up at two in the morning with a phone call? Will you help her and pray with her as she suffers and hurts and cries?

Do you love Jesus? Will you seek out the one whom you led to Christ six months ago but who now is sleeping with his girl-fiend? Or will you just look the other way and tell yourself in your most (un)convincing manner, "How can he do this to me after all I've done for him? The nerve . . ."

Quit protecting yourself. Let God take care of *all* your needs. Love someone. Take a risk, even a big one. Wash some wounds, dry some tears. Love someone. No, you won't do everything right, but that's okay. Just do it, do it and keep on doing it.

The good news of the gospel is that God draws straight lines with crooked sticks . . . like Gary, like you, like me.

There's a Paul somewhere in your life. Be a Gary. You must be a Gary. We need you.

he had a personal relationship with sin. He knew it, I knew it and God surely knew it. But unlike me, he had a thirsting desire to see more of Christ and less of sin as part of his life. He wanted to be godly—and he wanted me to be godly too.

I'll not soon forget that first time we prayed together. My first theology course took place in his den.

"Paul, Jesus is here in this room with us. See that empty chair in the corner? Picture Jesus being in that chair when we pray. He's really here in this room with us."

I gave him a funny look.

We got on our knees. We closed our eyes. He prayed. I peeked. He prayed again. I peeked again. I shrugged my shoulders. I would rest my faith in the counsel of the older brethren. I prayed.

God was indeed with Gary and me in that room. And in the days to come, my new life in Christ was not confined to Gary's den, nor was Christ confined to Gary's rocking chair. We got together weekly to read the Bible. We talked about God—and to him.

One week we would study the Bible with Ross, another fairly new Christian brother. Another week, we'd pray together with George, once my biggest competitor for class offices, lead roles in plays and certain girls on campus. Other times, we would enjoy the sunset on a warm spring evening at the nearby lake, as we shared problems and mutual concerns.

As numerous struggles continued in my life and new ones entered, Gary directed me to God as the one who was able and willing to meet my needs. And when he was burdened by his own struggles or unavailable for counsel, I was able to go to one of the other Christians I had gotten to know through him.

Long-Distance Support

I grew that summer after graduation. I was in a prayer group and hitchhiked a thousand miles with Gary to participate in a Young Life college prep camp—but inside I dreaded seeing

September roll around when Gary and I would be going to different schools.

I was the only student out of my high-school class who would be attending my college, and surely there would be no one in the thirteen thousand who would understand my Christian convictions and help me stick to them. Prior to this, my life had been literally controlled by one whim followed by two fancies, and I didn't want my faith in Jesus Christ to become just another one of those things I used to do.

College was everything I thought it would be . . . lousy, hard and lonely. My roommate felt I deserved three credits for the home correspondence course I seemed to be taking: I literally wrote two hundred and fifty letters to old high-school friends that first quarter. When I visited home two weeks after classes had begun, my friends greeted me with, "What took you so long?"

I majored in business because I thought it would make my father happy. It did until he saw my grades.

By January, I had conceded to the fact that I was the only Christian on campus. By March, that didn't concern me too much; I was more afraid that there soon would be no Christians on campus. The pressures of college had all but gotten to me. The word *defeated* was a complimentary way to describe my "victorious Christian life." My only real fellowship with other Christians was when I drove two hundred miles round trip to Gary's campus and participated in the gathering he had started with another believer.

But one thing happened in April that made a big difference. A very big difference.

All year long, some guys down the hall had been asking me to smoke dope with them. No, I'd tell them. Did Jesus ever smoke dope? Then neither could I. But by April, I wasn't too concerned about Jesus' welfare—only my own. I said yes one day, after bombing out on an important geometry test.

But right before going down the hall, I called Gary. I told him

what I was planning to do. He told me it was a[...] him I couldn't care less. He said he'd be right th[...] hung up on me. It was four in the afternoon. H[...] hundred miles and was there by seven. We tal[...] o'clock in the morning. For several hours we sat ag[...] of the architecture building, watching the rain s[...] before us, as I slowly, painfully and with great reli[...] deep hurts with him. He slept that night in the d[...] was back on the road by seven the next morning, [...] help of a trucker was in his nine o'clock class.

That was a turning point for me. God spoke [...] evening: I love you enough that I'll send a busy st[...] who needed to hit the books tonight, to let you k[...] uncertain terms that I hear you and am with you.

There was much comfort knowing I was not a six-[...] ect to Gary, and if I didn't live up to his expect[...] wouldn't drop me down a chute and say, "Who's next[...]

In future days, when I would be tempted to write[...] same God, to say he didn't really love me, strong men[...] that evening would make it impossible. The Word had[...] flesh. My relationship to the Lord improved after th[...] incident. As my trust in him grew, my devotional life im[...] I met other Christians (there actually were others!) and l[...] involved with the InterVarsity chapter. My roommate b[...] a Christian that spring.

My relationship to Gary continued to grow over the ne[...] years. Looking back, it's delightful to see how our conver[...] expanded from "How can I help you, Paul?" to "How ca[...] help the younger Christians in our schools grow?"

Through high school, through college and now as pr[...] sionals, our commitment to each other continues. I plan t[...] his friend until I die. And I know he feels the same com[...] ment.

He's in California and I'm in Florida; he's white and [...] Japanese-American; he's a businessman and I'm in Christi[...]

Attracted to Commitment

by Melissa Moskowitz

I *was scared. We had been told to wear heavy clothing and helmets* if we had them because our demonstration that day could potentially erupt into violence. We were going to march into Fort Dix in New Jersey to "free" some soldiers from the war machine.

We got off the chartered bus and quickly lined up in two columns of twenty-five each and marched two-by-two toward the fort's front gate. Facing us were ten soldiers with rifles. They slowly walked toward us as we marched into the fort and continued chanting our slogans.

All of a sudden, when we were about thirty yards away from the soldiers, smoke obscured our vision of them. "Tear gas!" someone yelled and soon we were all coughing and wheezing, our eyes burning. We scattered and quickly ran back out the way we had come in. But I knew that wouldn't be the last time I'd march for my beliefs.

For Peace But without Peace

My father was the first to instill in me the power and value of commitment. I remember a cold winter morning when I was in elementary school seeing my father walk in the door, haggard and bleary-eyed from an all-night vigil in Harlem, a Black ghetto of Manhattan. He and his comrades had strapped themselves to a bulldozer to protest the building of a state office which would cause the eviction of a number of people from their homes. My father instilled in me the awareness that there are causes which are worthy of our time and that could cost us the respect and acceptance of others. He taught me the meaning of commitment.

By the time I entered college I was well on my way to becoming a social activist myself. I was drawn into the growing peace movement and rallied alongside others who believed we could effect change if we marched and shouted loud enough.

During my first years in college I was so involved that I risked flunking out. Repeatedly we protested on campus and tried to get the school to shut down. We also took several trips to Washington to protest our government's foreign policy.

But one day, at the height of my involvement, something happened that made me wonder about the frenzy of my commitment. We had been marching for many hours with several thousand other students in the nation's capital and were resting in a classroom in a nearby university, talking about the day's events. But our rest didn't last long—once again we were tear gassed.

I felt so indignant as we scrambled out with burning eyes. All this time I had thought we were doing the right thing but everything seemed in vain. As we quietly got in the car and went home, I told myself that I was tired of all the noise, all the slogans, all our anger. Despite our fervor, peace was as far off a reality as ever, and we just couldn't bring it about. Nobody seemed to be listening.

Doubt began to fall over me like a slow but certain nightfall.

My commitment to our cause had cost me sore feet and a hoarse voice; it had cost me time and even caused my grades to suffer. It had even endangered me physically. But it had wrought no change. So why continue?

During the next year I gave up my involvement in the peace movement, and I decided to get more serious about school. I became an art student, committed to seeing life through the eyes of Rembrandt and Picasso. I felt at home within the small art community at my college. It was there that I discovered another group of committed people.

A New Kind of Radical

One day Joseph, a friend in one of my classes, told me that Jesus was the Jewish Messiah. Being raised in a Jewish home, I thought this was a radical statement for a Jew to make. I took a good look at Joseph; he certainly seemed normal. He didn't look like a fanatic, but he definitely was one. He was as committed to his belief in Jesus as I had been to my belief in the peace movement. But there was something different about his belief: his brought him peace.

It also compelled him to share that faith with me. And that bothered me.

Joseph read the Bible quite seriously and witnessed to everyone he met—my family included. His friends made fun of him, and his own family was incensed about his conversion. "You're never going to amount to very much if you continue in this!" his father would yell at him. I also found out that he was going out on the streets and handing out literature to people and being verbally abused for his faith.

I became attracted to Jesus, albeit reluctantly, because I had known Joseph and his friends before when they had been heavily into drugs. The changes I'd seen in them challenged me.

Hours of debate, where they often would point out prophetic Scriptures in the Old Testament which seemed to point to Jesus, increased my desire to find out more about him. Since I had already decided to take a semester off from school to sort things out, I used the opportunity to read the Bible and explore this person who was invading my life. It was a disturbing time. A book that I had considered closed to me for so long all of a sudden wasn't so closed. *But how could all this be true if I had never heard of it before?* I would ask myself.

But I kept coming back to the commitment of my friends. If they hadn't been so given to the cause I wouldn't have persisted in seeking Jesus. I too wanted to be committed to something that would last. And I wanted the closeness and the joy they were experiencing. For a while I thought if I could act like them but not become a Christian it would be great. But I wasn't able to pull that off.

Whenever I would be about to accept Jesus I would come out of it by saying, "But Jewish people don't believe in Jesus!" Yet, it couldn't be true, for several of my friends were Jewish.

The thing about my involvement in the peace movement was that I really wanted to see peace. I was beginning to see that believing in Jesus was the answer to the emptiness I had felt in Washington.

The Cost of Commitment

In time, God gave me the strength and grace to make a personal commitment to Christ. The day I made my decision, I burst into our apartment and shouted, "I'm saved, I'm saved!"

"What are you talking about?" my sister retorted. I told them. My answer didn't go over very big.

My father was angry that I had become so closed-minded and my mother was horrified that my Jewish upbringing now seemed to be for nought. And as I got more committed to Jesus I could see their respect for me melting away.

I had to get used to whispers behind my back at family gatherings. And later, when I got married, most of my relatives did not attend my wedding ceremony because they did not want to hear about our "religion."

This pain was mixed in with the joy I was experiencing in my new relationship with Jesus. I saw changes in my own heart. For example, I was able to make difficult decisions because I had something important to base them on. I had been studying dance, but for the first time I was able to see the ungodly competition of the dance world. So I quit. Before I became a believer in Jesus, the issue wouldn't even have fazed me.

I was so excited I talked to anyone I could about the Lord. This time I saw that my fervency brought changes as I saw others turn their lives to Jesus.

As time went on, I felt called by God to make a full-time commitment to the work of Jews for Jesus. This greatly disappointed my family, because this more public expression of my faith brought them further embarrassment. Plus they felt I could be "making something more" of my life.

Despite my peace demonstration days, nothing prepared me for the rejection I've encountered as a missionary with Jews for Jesus. I've participated in four summer evangelistic campaigns, where I've stood on busy, city street corners and handed out our gospel tracts. I never felt so vulnerable in my life! People who didn't even know the first thing about me passed by and felt free to call me names, shout at me and sometimes try to physically stop me from what I was doing.

One afternoon an angry young man pulled the tracts out of my hand and threw them on the sidewalk. I would think, *If they only knew me, they would know what a nice person I am!*

And so the early example of my father has come full circle to me. My faith and commitment to the God of our fathers has cost me the acceptance of those dearest to me. Sometimes it hurts so much I am tempted to compromise what I believe so I can be accepted once again. Yet God continues to be there for me.

Several years ago Jews for Jesus demonstrated in San Francisco in front of a night-club strip joint named *Garden of Eden.*

The fifteen of us, marching with our "Love not Lust" and "Jesus Loves You" pickets, got a lot of ridicule. Passersby shouted obscenities and the huge bouncers meanly stared us down.

The biggest difference between this demonstration and the times at Fort Dix and Washington was that I knew that what I believed in could change people's hearts even if the externals, such as the strip joint, never changed. *Peace at last!*

Encounter with Power

by Rob Decker with Andrés Tapia

I *work with a campus fellowship group. Together we had spent* most of the year aggressively evangelizing through booktables, dorm talks, knocking on doors and investigative Bible studies. And every one of us was burned out. We had worked so hard and yet we had seen few results. No one wanted to do evangelism next year, including me.

Yet during the last few months of our frustrating school year, I began to experience a different method of evangelism that was to transform our outreach and our impact on campus.

I had been rereading the Gospels, trying to understand how Jesus did evangelism. And I noticed that a lot of his evangelism was accompanied by manifestations of power. I began to wonder if that stuff could happen today. Over the next several months as I studied the Scriptures, talked to pastors and read other books, there seemed to be no indication why it couldn't. Eventually I found myself asking God to present me with opportunities to see his power in action.

What's in a Name?

One of the first times God answered this prayer was when I got talking to a man near campus about Jesus. I tried to convince him of Jesus' validity by using some of the best apologetics I know. But I got nowhere. In frustration, I prayed to God, *I'm stuck! None of my arguments are working. What should I do? Help!* At that moment, the name *Calvin* popped into my mind. Calvin? *What does that have to do with anything?* Since I didn't know anyone by that name, I couldn't figure out why the name kept coming to mind. As our conversation came to an end, it dawned on me that the name could be significant to Jim, the man I was talking to. I had that feeling of when, for some unexplainable reason, you get the urge to call someone and when you do they say, "I can't believe you called! I was desperate and I needed to talk to you." So I asked him, "Uh, does the name *Calvin* mean anything to you?"

He turned a bit pale and his eyes opened up really wide. "He used to be my best buddy." My heart skipped a beat. "He was also an alcoholic. When we were in California he became a Christian during a church service he had walked into . . ." By this point, *my* eyes, and mouth, were opened wide. ". . . and now, several years later, he's a pastor." With great suspicion, he wanted to know how I had known his buddy's name. I didn't know what to answer! I finally told him that I thought God had placed it in my head. And then I felt the prompting to add, "And God wants you to know that if he can change Calvin's life, he can change yours too."

I never saw Jim again, but that experience led to many other similar experiences. Things would come to my mind that revealed something about the person that I couldn't have known. During that period I found myself reading over and over the story of the woman at the well (Jn 4:17-18). To my embarrassment, there were many times when I said something and it was wrong and I would feel foolish. But the more I took risks, the better I seemed to get at discerning what seemed to be from

God and what was my own imagination.

Beyond Embarrassment

I then started to offer to pray for people's needs, whether physical or emotional, right there on the spot. At first nothing much seemed to happen, except that usually the person was touched that I had taken the time to show I cared. I started to get so excited about these encounters that I suggested to my students that they try it. They thought I was crazy, but at the same time they were intrigued.

Over the next few months we studied the Scriptures, especially where they related to Jesus' ministry. We talked about it a lot and eventually a few wanted to start being open to possibilities. But they were scared to death. It seemed too risky. "What if nothing happens?" they would ask me. Especially after our previous frustration, no one wanted more of the same.

Some, however, began to step out and be bold. Carlos, a senior majoring in mechanical engineering, was one of the first. He told me this story:

"The girl at the checkout counter at my dorm dining hall was complaining of a headache. I went, sat down and had dinner. Then I mustered up some courage and went over to her and asked her if I could pray for her headache. She said sure. I said, 'Yeah, uh, but I'd like to do it right here.' She looked at me as if I was weird. I gave her a weak smile, because I felt the same way about myself, but I put my hand on her forehead and prayed that the headache would go away. When I took my hand away, she looked at me puzzled and said 'It's gone.' I couldn't believe it! I was so freaked out and so was she that we didn't know what to say to each other. 'Why did you do it?' she finally blurted out. Well, this led to lots of good discussions about the Lord over the next few months."

It wasn't to be the last time God would use Carlos in a special way. That experience pumped him up, and he kept praying for similar opportunities. It also encouraged others in the group to be a bit more bold.

Brad, a junior electrical-engineering major, seized an opportunity in his fraternity room with three non-Christian friends—frat brothers Dan and Cary, and his friend Daphne. Cary was complaining about a boil on his right ankle. Brad asked, "Can I pray for it?" Daphne, instead of Cary, responded, "You want to do *what!* That's the stupidest thing I ever heard of."

Brad, somewhat shaken by Daphne's response, explained to them why he believed that praying for Cary's boil was something very legitimate. Daphne didn't like the answer and left in a huff. But Dan and Cary stayed, intrigued by the whole idea.

Brad placed his hand over the boil while both Cary and Dan looked on. He prayed that God would take the boil away. After a few seconds Cary excitedly said he felt some heat around the boil. They looked and it was half gone! Now all three got very excited. "Let's pray some more," Brad said. After a few more minutes of prayer they all looked and the boil was completely gone! Everyone was so amazed that again no one knew what to say. Finally Dan asked, "Can you pray for my headache?" Brad did but nothing happened. Afterward, however, Dan said "While you were praying for me I really felt loved."

Dan and Cary then went looking for Daphne and showed her the spot where the boil had been. She was flabbergasted and immediately went to Brad's room and peppered him with questions about God and his power.

Reading about Jesus' ministry in the Gospels took on more immediate meaning for these students after their initial "power encounters." It was clear that Jesus did preach, had good friendship-evangelism encounters and fed the hungry, but that he also operated in power. And when we read John 14:11-12, it clinched the validity of what we were beginning to experience: "Believe me when I say that I am in the Father and the Father is in me; or at least believe on the evidence of the miracles themselves. I tell you the truth, anyone who has faith in me will do what I have been doing. He will do even greater things than these, because I am going to the Father."

Both the Scriptures and the experiences of their friends were encouraging more students to take risks. While Penny, a communications-studies junior, was praying for Liz, a very needy person in her drama class, *One Hundred and One Dalmatians* came to her mind. Wondering if it was something she ate, Penny didn't think much of it, though the image stayed with her the rest of the day. Later, while she was knocking on doors inviting people to a Bible study, her heart quickened when she noticed that one door had a *One Hundred and One Dalmatians* note board. Penny knocked on the door, but no one was in. Even so, because of the coincidence, Penny left a note on the board inviting the room's occupant to the Bible study. That person showed up at Penny's Bible study—it was Liz.

Liz was shocked when Penny told her what had happened. She didn't know God could be so real and could direct people in such concrete ways.

Meanwhile Carlos was continuing to pray for the guys in his dorm every chance he got. Once, during a break from homework, he thought he saw Chris, a sophomore history major he didn't know very well who lived across the hall from him, walk into his room wearing a Joliet Catholic High School jacket. Carlos didn't think much of it until a few days later when he sat with Chris at the cafeteria.

In the midst of the conversation Carlos casually asked, "So you went to a Catholic high school?"

The guy was floored. "Who told you that?" he said a bit defensively. "No one here knows that."

Carlos explained to him he had seen him wearing the jacket in the dorm and described what the jacket looked like. Chris was utterly confused. "But I don't even have the jacket here. It's back at my folks' home in Joliet."

Carlos by then had figured out that something powerful had happened, and he explained to his friend how God sometimes gives visions to help bring people to himself.

"From that point on," says Carlos, "he became very receptive to the gospel, often stopping by my room to talk about God." That summer Chris committed his life to Christ.

The students were finding out that talking about Jesus with some non-Christians became a lot easier once they had experienced the power of God in their lives. Not that this was necessary all, or even most, of the time, but it sure opened up opportunities that it seems wouldn't have happened otherwise.

By spring quarter of that year, many of the Christians in the group were doing evangelism this way. The stories they shared with each other really gave them confidence that amazing things could happen if they simply took the risks. They also enjoyed telling each other the times when nothing happened. Being able to laugh about it helped take away the sting of the embarrassment, but it also helped them see that consistently, regardless of the result, their friendship with a non-Christian would be strengthened.

Keeping Power in Perspective

These are only a few of the countless stories that happened that year and continue today. Evangelism has taken on a very different meaning for us. We did a lot of processing during this time, especially studying how all that we were experiencing jibed with Scripture. Some of our conclusions:

Power encounters were not the end-all of evangelism. We continued in apologetics, open-air preaching, investigative Bible studies. But what we found was that on many occasions people's encounter with power opened them up to participating in one of these events. A lot of the students and myself were good at apologetics, but we rarely saw anyone come to Christ that way. We found out that many people didn't just want a philosophy to believe in, they wanted something they knew was real. These power encounters often provided just that. I also found that because these power encounters increased our faith, it also made us more effective at the other forms of evangelism, such as apologetics and other planned events.

We also realized that even when people experience God's touch, they don't necessarily turn to him. A good biblical precedent was the nine lepers in Luke 17:15-19. And with many cases we would never find out how God ended up using the experience in the person's life. Others seemed as antagonistic as ever. Daphne recently wrote "God Is Dead" on a sidewalk on campus.

Another thing that proved important was the way we treated the people receiving prayer. We would never accuse them of not having enough faith. We would just shrug our shoulders, since we still felt we had a lot to learn, and leave the results up to God. And we never told anyone not to go to a doctor or take their medicine. We believed that those things were also God-given for the healing of the sick.

It was an exciting year. And the students are now hooked on evangelism. We all know that we have a lot more to learn about God's touch of power, but the changed lives we saw will be something we'll never forget.

A floormate of Carlos's summed up the essence of what we had discovered. He was contrasting Carlos's faith with that of a Hindu they had initially been impressed with because of his discipline of daily morning devotions. He said, "Carlos put his faith into action while the Hindu guy never did anything for us. Not only that, but Carlos's God really healed and touched people!"

Campus Casualty: A Parable

by Stephen Board

Mike *hit campus two years ago as your usual confident* atheist. He had a warm, atheistic home life. He was trained in an atheist high school, armed with the atheist catechism. But Mike lost his faith in college.

Things began to get wobbly right away during freshman orientation. Mike met his roommate who turned out to be one of those religious people. Wilf, the roommate, got things going by moving in a Bible, a catchy religious poster and a big box of theological books.

"I've heard about people like you," Wilf said. "But I've never met one. Maybe you can explain your beliefs to me sometime."

That night, while Wilf was away, Mike reviewed the techniques in a book he had brought, *How to Give Away Your Unbelief.* It dealt with answering religious people's questions, getting conversations going, what to do when a religious person wants to say a prayer before a meal—that sort of thing.

It was kind of funny, the way Mike and Wilf swapped propaganda. Mike gave Wilf a copy of *The God Who Is Not There,* and Wilf gave Mike a copy of *Why I Am Not an Atheist.*

In class the pressure was really on. Mike never felt more uncomfortable as an atheist. Back in atheist high, he had learned a pack of arguments for the nonexistence of God. Science, he had learned, supported materialism. Literature supported secularism. Psychology translated all your beliefs into conditioning. But here at college Mike learned how parochial an atheistic high school can be.

Zoology, for example. The zo prof got loads of mileage out of the design of animal life on earth, right down to the genetic chemistry. "I'll bet some of you have the childish idea that all this just happened," the prof chortled. Seemed like the whole class cracked up in horse laughs. "Now that you are at the university you may as well grow up. Part of your education is in learning reasons for things and not copping out with explanations like "chance." Mike was glad when the semester ended.

In literature Mike felt safe. He had memorized a few poems of unbelief and had read some profound atheistic novels back in high school. William Ernest Henley's *Invictus* was one of his favorites. But freshmen introductory lit revised everything. Mike's assigned research project was a comparison of John Donne and Gerard Manley Hopkins, two poets who believed in you-know-Who. His paper was charged, so to speak, with the grandeur of God.

Prose was not much better. God lurked everywhere, from readings in the Bible and Augustine to Samuel Johnson, Tolstoy and Dostoyevsky.

The same story in history. He had always thought an atheist ruler would be more enlightened and humane than one who believed in God or gods. That seemed to make sense as they studied the Inquisition and the religious wars. But the twentieth century shot the theory to pieces: all that bloodshed under atheistic dictators.

At the end of his freshman year, our hero was ready to drop

out of university and transfer to a private atheistic college. The year had worn him down. "My God, what's happening to me?" he mumbled, as he crossed the quad to avoid an outdoor rally promoting the reality of God.

The summer helped him recover: home with the folks, the old friends, the familiar hometown with its familiar disbelief in God. True, some of those people bugged him. The family Atheist Adviser was a hypocrite, and Mike's own atheistic parents were not all they ought to be. But by the end of the summer, he felt up to another year at the U.

Well, sometime that winter, between Christmas and the Day of the Rising Son (that's what people on campus were calling Easter), Mike went over to the Other Side, joined the God people and installed a sky in his world.

It seems his doubts about atheism had increased for months before he finally packed it all in.

His psych classes had taught him to criticize his beliefs. "I'm a child of atheist parents and the product of an atheist background; I've never thought it through for myself." Another thing that bothered him was, "What about all the people who have never heard of atheism? They seem to get along okay without changing their beliefs." But the big thing was the problem of evil. "What about all the suffering in the world? If there is no God, injustice will never be put right—it just goes on and on, evil heaped on evil and never judged."

Mike wrote a letter describing his conversion to a high-school friend. "It was like the sun coming out," he wrote. "Here at school I could see God make sense the more I thought about him. I feel like I've grown up . . . or maybe just been born."

What's the Message?

Evangelistic Snapshot

I sat next to a Black law student on a bus to Salem, Oregon. She was an avowed Marxist who felt that if we lived in a classless society we would be freed of the things that weigh us down.

After she was done explaining her philosophy, I asked her: "I know a guy. He is one of the worst racists I have ever met. If he lived with you for fifty years in your classless society, every time he saw you he'd still call you 'nigger.' How can Marx wipe out the ugliness and hatred of a bigot?"

She turned away from me, her eyes glaring, and, looking out the window she said, "Right on. We've been trying to change that for centuries. And all the rules and laws in the world can't change you. The laws curb behavior, they can force you to treat me justly, but they can't make you love me."

I knew I had struck a raw nerve. "You're saying that the real evil comes from within us. So you need a system that regards evil as internal and a solution that transforms radically, not curbs superficially. Right?"

"Yeah, well it'll take more than a human attempt to change us that much. But we need it," she said.

"I couldn't agree more. In fact that's the very kind of system I've found," I said.

"Really? Hey, what revolution are you into?"

After she recovered from her shock that I followed Jesus, she asked me how I knew it was true. For the rest of the trip she asked me to defend Christianity—and she listened intently.

When we arrived she said, "I'd like to get together again. And there's something you're not going to believe. When I went home this weekend, my younger sister told me she'd become a Christian. I told her it was anti-intellectual and unsubstantiated. In a furor I packed my bags, walked out saying I never wanted to discuss it again, got on the bus and sat down next to you."

—Becky Pippert in *Out of the Saltshaker* (IVP).

First Steps to God: An Outline

Here is an outline that summarizes the main points of the gospel in four words: *God, Man, Christ, Response.* To be faithful to the gospel, we must convey the vital truth clustering around each of these words.

God

God loves you (Jn 3:16).

God is holy and just and too pure to look on evil (Hab 1:13a). He punishes all evil (Rom 1:18).

Man

God, who created everything, made us for himself to find our purpose in fellowship with him (Col 1:16).

But we rebelled and turned away from God (Is 53:6). The result is separation from God (Is 59:2). The penalty is eternal death (Rom 6:23).

Christ

God became a human being in the person of Jesus Christ to restore the broken fellowship (Col 1:19-20). Christ lived a perfect life (1 Pet 2:22).

Christ died as a substitute for us by paying the death penalty for our rebellion (Rom 5:8). He arose and is alive today to give us a new life of fellowship with God, now and forever (1 Cor 15:3-4; Jn 3:16; 10:10).

Response

I must repent for my rebellion (Mt 4:17).

I must believe Christ died to provide forgiveness and a new life of fellowship with God (Jn 1:12).

I must receive Christ as my Savior and Lord with the intent to obey him. I do this in prayer by inviting him into my life (Rev 3:20).

Is Jesus God? An Otherworldly Debate

by Peter Kreeft

P resident John F. Kennedy and author C. S. Lewis both died on the same day—an especially interesting fact given their diametrically opposed world views. Lewis was a champion of the Western theistic viewpoint and John F. Kennedy based his leadership style on the Western humanist view. To give us a glimpse of the issues involved in presenting the gospel, Peter Kreeft has put together a fictitious debate between these two great twentieth-century minds.

Kennedy: I just can't buy that old-fashioned theology of God descending from heaven like a meteor.

C. S. Lewis: All right, then, who is Jesus, according to your faith?

Kennedy: The ideal man, the man so perfect and wise that his followers called him divine. Not God become man but man become God.

Lewis: A very nicely put summary of humanist Christology; but do you think this is *Christianity*?

Kennedy: Old Christianity, no; New Christianity, yes. The only form of it a modern man can believe without giving up his intellectual honesty. I heard a preacher put it this way: you can be honest, or intelligent, or a medieval-style Christian, or any two of the three, but not all three. Work that out for yourself.

Lewis: Very clever, but the same barb can be used to sting anyone. I can say you can be honest, or intelligent, or a modernist, or any two of the three, but not all three. The substantive point, as distinct from the debater's nicety, is the identity of Jesus. Let's zero in on that issue.

Kennedy: Fine. Who is Jesus?

Lewis: God become man.

Kennedy: Literally?

Lewis: Yes.

Kennedy: How can you as an educated twentieth-century man take such an outdated position?

Lewis: As distinct from your new, modern one?

Kennedy: Yes.

Lewis: Because for one thing, your new position is as old as the hills. Or, at least, as old as Arius.

Kennedy: Who?

Lewis: Arius, a fourth-century heretic who carried half the church with him, even after the Council of Nicea addressed the issue by clearly and strongly affirming Jesus' divinity. The same thing is happening again today with modernism and humanism. Your so-called New Christianity is nothing but the old Arian heresy in new dress.

Kennedy: Really, now, there's no need to call each other names.

Lewis: I didn't call you a name; I just labeled your position accurately.

Kennedy: I wish you would avoid using labels like *heresy*. They're so . . . so outdated. So unenlightened. So medieval. So primitive.

Lewis: Jack, when I want to disprove an idea, I try to prove that it is false. Your argument against my idea that your belief was a heresy was simply that my idea was old. *Outdated,* I believe you said. *Medieval* and *primitive* were two more of your terms. Those are all words about age, not truth.

Kennedy: All right, my friend. If you want to be so logical, I challenge you: prove to me logically that Jesus is God and not just man.

Lewis: All right.

Kennedy: What?

Lewis: I just said, "All right." Why the surprise?

Kennedy: I thought you were going to say something about mysteries and faith and authority and the church. Do you mean you are going to try to *reason* yourself into the old faith?

Lewis: Not myself; I'm already there. But you, perhaps.

Kennedy: Did you reason yourself into it? Did you arrive at your belief by reason alone?

Lewis: Reason *alone*? Of course not. But I looked before I leaped. I reasoned before I believed. And *after* I believed too— I mean, once I believed, I was convinced by the way reason backed up faith. It couldn't prove everything but it could give strong arguments for many things.

Kennedy: How could you ever prove he is alive and immortal and divine? You are a mere man, reasoning with mere words about an invisible and absent person who died centuries ago.

Lewis: The only answer is the proof itself. The only way to prove that a thing can be proved is to prove it.

Kennedy: Prove it then. No more diversions.

Lewis: Aut deus aut homo malus.

Kennedy: What? Are we speaking in tongues now, or what?

Lewis: That's my proof, or its summary. It's Latin for . . .

Kennedy: I know. I was just kidding. "Either God or a bad man." Now how is that a proof?

Lewis: Let's go through the logic of it. The first premise is that Christ must be either God, as he claims to be, or a bad man, if he isn't who he claims to be. The second premise is that he isn't a bad man. The conclusion is that he is God.

Kennedy: The logical form seems to be correct, but why must

I accept either premise?

Lewis: As for the second premise, even his opponents do not usually say he was a bad man. They try to make out that he was only a good man whom his disciples "divinized." But the first premise states that "just a good man" is the one thing he could not possibly be.

Kennedy: Why? Prove the first premise. That's the nub of the argument. The second is a platitude.

Lewis: Right. Consider this: Christ claimed to be the "Son of God." Remember what that implies.

Kennedy: What?

Lewis: What is the primary thing a father gives to his son?

Kennedy: Love, I suppose.

Lewis: Try again.

Kennedy: Education? caring? time?

Lewis: All those can be given only if the primary gift is given first.

Kennedy: You mean existence.

Lewis: Yes. And what kind of existence?

Kennedy: Human existence, of course.

Lewis: Yes. Human existence, human life, human nature. Human parents give humanity to their children. And what do oyster parents give to their oyster children?

Kennedy: Oyster nature.

Lewis: And wolf parents give wolf nature to their wolf children. And Martian parents give Martian nature. So the son of an oyster is what?

Kennedy: An oyster.

Lewis: And the son of a wolf is . . .

Kennedy: A wolf. And the son of a Martian is a Martian.

Lewis: And the Son of God?

Kennedy: I see. The title does seem to imply divinity, doesn't it? But I've heard that the term son of God is sometimes used in Scripture to refer to creatures. Angels are called sons of God in some places, and all Christians are called sons of God.

Lewis: Shall we review some of the other things Jesus said that more clearly claim divinity?

Kennedy: Before we look at that, I'd like to be clear about the logic of the argument. Suppose Jesus did claim divinity. That doesn't prove he was divine. Lots of people claim things that aren't theirs.

Lewis: But a mere man who claimed to be God would not be a good man, don't you see?

Kennedy: Hmmm. What would he be, according to your thinking?

Lewis: A bad man, just as the argument says.

Kennedy: Suppose he was just confused?

Lewis: Then he was intellectually bad. You see, he either believes his claim to be God, or he doesn't. If he does, then he is intellectually bad—very bad, in fact, because that's a pretty large confusion! And if he does not believe his claim, then he is morally bad: a deceiver and a terrible blasphemer.

Kennedy: So what are all the possibilities?

Lewis: An intellectually bad man, a morally bad man, a good man or God. In other words, insane, blasphemer, nice guy or God. And the one of those four that he couldn't possibly be is the third. But that's what you and millions of other humanists think he was.

Kennedy: The argument is just too neat. I simply can't stomach that kind of black-and-white thinking.

Lewis: That is an interesting psychological fact about your personal temperament, but it doesn't refute my argument, you know. You don't answer an argument by saying you don't like it, or don't like arguments, or can't stomach clarity.

Kennedy: What I want to say is this: how can you talk about a person in such stark, extreme alternative categories?

Lewis: With him, you have to. He forces you to one of two extreme positions by his claim, the most extreme claim anyone ever made.

Kennedy: But Lewis, could you review some of the claims for divinity that Jesus made? I think we should get our data straight first, before interpreting it. What, exactly, did he say about himself?

Lewis: All right. Taking the texts as they stand, let's gather the data. Here are some quotations: "I and the Father are one." "He who has seen me has seen the Father." "I am the resurrection and the life; he who believes in me, though he die, yet shall he live, and whoever lives and believes in me shall never die." "I am the bread of life." "I am the way and the truth and the life; no one comes to the Father but by me." "Your sins are forgiven."

Kennedy: Wait a minute. How is that last statement a claim to divinity? I'd want to forgive others' sins too. And didn't he command us to forgive one another?

Lewis: Yes, for sins against yourself I'm sure you could forgive someone who may have insulted you, for instance. But suppose you forgave him for insulting me?

Kennedy: That would be asinine.

Lewis: Quite. Do you see what it would be assuming?

Kennedy: Whoever forgives assumes he has the right to forgive.

Lewis: Yes, and who has the right to forgive an offender?

Kennedy: The one offended.

Lewis: Exactly. So Jesus' claim to forgive all sins assumed that he was the one offended in all sins. And who is that?

Kennedy: I see. God. The author of the moral law. Well, can you prove your second premise, that Jesus was not a bad man, not insane?

Lewis: If I do, you know what follows, don't you?

Kennedy: What do you mean?

Lewis: Why, we've already proved the first premise: Jesus must be either God or a bad man. If we also prove the second premise, that Jesus is not a bad man, then you must accept the conclusion that he is God.

Kennedy: I think I'm beginning to see why I want to avoid logic. But go on. Prove the second premise.

Lewis: Very well. Let's divide humanity first into the few enormously great and wise people like Jesus, Buddha, Socrates, Lao-Tzu, Moses, Mohammed, Confucius, Zoroaster . . .

Kennedy: I get you. You needn't go on with the list. But the dividing line between these few and the many is a soft one, not a hard one, you understand?

Lewis: I understand. Let's call these few the sages, and the vast majority of the human race that are left the non-sages. Although it is true, as you say, that the dividing line is soft, that wisdom is a matter of degree rather than a black-or-white quality, yet we can and do single out a few as extraordinarily wise, can we not?

Kennedy: Yes. So far you have two classes. You said you were going to divide people into four.

Lewis: Right. Let's also divide people into those who claim to be the God the Bible talks about, and all those who do not.

Kennedy: Do you mean to say now that there is only one member to the first class? Only one man who claimed to be God? Is that going to be your point?

Lewis: Not at all. There are a number of such people, though you have probably never met one.

Kennedy: Where are they?

Lewis: Most of them are in insane asylums.

Kennedy: Oh. Yes. The "divinity complex."

Lewis: It is at least common enough to merit that technical term, and a paragraph or two in manuals of abnormal psychology. Now let's combine the two divisions and get our four classes of people:

First, there are those who neither claim to be God nor are remarkably wise—the vast majority of us.

Second, there are those who do not claim to be God and are remarkably wise—people like Buddha, Socrates, Confucius, Lao-Tzu, Moses, Mohammed and the rest.

Third, there are those who claim to be God and are not remarkably wise—the insane.

Fourth, there are those who both claim to be God and are remarkably wise.

Kennedy: And whom do you put into Class Four?

Lewis: Only one.

Kennedy: I thought so.

Lewis: Can you think of another?

Kennedy: No. But this classification alone does not prove Jesus' claim to divinity is true.

Lewis: No, but it amplifies and explains the premise of the *aut deus aut homo malus* proof. Only two kinds of men claim to be God, and one kind is a bad man, not a sage.

Kennedy: So what is the logic of the argument now? You still haven't proven the divinity of Jesus.

Lewis: Into which of the following three classes would you put him? Ordinary people, sages or pseudo gods?

Kennedy: Sages, of course.

Lewis: No, for they do not claim to be God, and he does.

Kennedy: Hmmm. Suppose we try pseudo gods?

Lewis: No, because they lack the wisdom, compassion and creativity that he has.

Kennedy: And not ordinary people, because . . .

Lewis: For both reasons. There is only one possibility left. How can it be avoided?

Kennedy: And that is?

Lewis: He is a sage, therefore to be trusted. And he claims to be God; therefore he is not just another human sage. There you have it: either God or a bad man.

Kennedy: The conclusion seems to follow if you accept the premises. But the first form of the argument seems weaker. I think I can still quarrel with that. The premise "either a bad man or God" is the black-and-white thinking I'm still suspicious of.

Lewis: That's where my fourfold classification comes in. It proves that either/or premise.

Kennedy: How?

Lewis: There are only four possibilities. He is either God, or a bad man (blasphemous or insane), or a good man (a mere sage), or an ordinary man. That's another way of stating the either/or premise, with four possibilities instead of two. And you can't classify Jesus in any one of the other three categories.

Kennedy: The conclusion seems to follow here too. Yet I don't want to be forced to admit that.

Lewis: Why not? If the argument really proves it, then it must be true. Don't you want to admit what's true?

Kennedy: Of course. But there must be something wrong with the argument.

Lewis: Why?

Kennedy: Well, I don't want to accept the conclusion.

Lewis: Do your wants determine the truth?

Kennedy: No, but I don't believe the conclusion is true.

Lewis: But if you cannot refute the argument, you must.

Kennedy: Must I, really? Why? I think I'm being bullied.

Lewis: By the truth, not by me. If you cannot refute the argument, you can mean only one thing by refusing the conclusion.

Kennedy: What?

Lewis: That you know it's true and still refuse to believe it; that you simply don't care about truth; that you don't want to know the truth. In short, that you are dishonest.

Kennedy: How dare you? I've not been dishonest with you. I've been quite candid.

Lewis: Yes, and I appreciate that. But you'd be dishonest with reality if you admitted that the argument proves the conclusion to be true and you still refuse to believe it. I don't think you are dishonest; that's why you will have to accept the conclusion. Why don't you want to believe it?

Kennedy: What do you mean? I just don't believe it, that's all.

For the fuller scope of this conversation (which also included Eastern pantheist Aldous Huxley), pick up a copy of Between Heaven and Hell *by Peter Kreeft (IVP), from which this chapter was adapted.*

Is Jesus the Only Way?

by Darrell Johnson

Why is it that we disciples of Jesus Christ find it so difficult to name his name in our world? We freely share our feelings about the Middle Eastern struggle, the latest film or the way the president handles the economy. We can even talk to others about our latest romance. But when it comes to talking to others about Jesus, we hold back. Why? One word: *fear.* We fear people's reactions to what we will say about Jesus. We fear being judged by others as being old-fashioned or narrow-minded and intolerant, or as needing a crutch.

Why would discussing Jesus Christ provoke such reactions? Because the good news of Jesus Christ, though it's the best news you'll ever hear, is also offensive news. Not only does the gospel say that Jesus saves, that he makes all things new, that he forgives and cleanses and makes broken people whole; the gospel also says that only Jesus saves, that only he can make all things new, that only he can finally forgive and cleanse and make us whole.

These words ruffle feathers in our pluralistic society. "What do you mean, *only* Jesus? How can you, a mere human in one little corner of the globe, say there is no other name by which we must be saved? What about *Krishna, Buddha, Mohammed* or *Marx?* What about the salvation promised by Eckankar, est or Scientology?"

As long as we Christians say that Jesus is one of many saviors, we are warmly welcomed at the religious smorgasbord. We are welcomed even if we say that Jesus is the greatest of all the candidates for savior. But once we muster up the courage to say that Jesus is the only savior the world has, we are asked to leave the table.

Who's on Trial?

During Peter and John's trial in Acts, Peter said, "Salvation is found in no one else" (4:12). They also said that the lame man they had prayed for had been healed by Jesus, whom these same accusers had crucified. Notice how the roles in that trial changed. Peter and John were no longer on trial. Jesus was on trial. How ironic! The Jewish leaders who were interrogating Peter and John were the same ones who interrogated Jesus the night before he was executed. They were being given a chance to reverse their previous verdict. But once again they decided to send Jesus away. Once again they came to the verdict that Jesus was not who he claimed to be. And they ordered Peter and John never again to speak in Jesus' name.

Read Acts to see what effect that order had! It was like ordering the earth to stop spinning. Peter and John had found life and salvation in Jesus; and they knew that that life, that salvation, was available to any and all who came to Jesus; and they knew that that life, that salvation, was found *only* in Jesus. They had to keep on speaking in the name of Jesus regardless of the consequences.

"Salvation is found in no one else" is the message the risen Christ asks us to bring to our campuses. And we simply have to accept the fact that this message, this gospel, offends any group that doesn't like absolutes. We have to accept the scandal of particularity—the biblical claim that God has fully revealed himself in one particular person, Jesus of Nazareth, and that God has decisively acted to save the world in this man and only in him.

The world rightly asks, "Why? Why is there no other name by which we can be saved?"

Before answering that question, let's be clear about what we are *not* claiming when we say "there is no other name."

All Truth Is God's
First of all, when we say there is no other name, we are not saying there is no truth in other names. Every culture and religion has some expression of God's truth. Part of the evangelistic task of the church is to search out those truths and show how the gospel of Jesus Christ relates to them. To claim there is no other name but Jesus does not mean other religions and philosophies do not speak any truth. It is, however, to claim that those truths are to be reassessed in the light of Jesus Christ who claims to be the Truth (Jn 14:6).

Second, when we say there is no other name, we are not saying that we can't learn from other names. Christians can learn a great deal from the rest of the world. The intensity with which a Hindu seeks God can make us look like hypocrites. The discipline of a Muslim can make us look very lazy. The total commitment of a Marxist can put us to shame. We have much to learn from people of other faiths and philosophies.

Third, when we say there is no other name, we are not saying that Christianity is the one true religion. Peter was not making any claims for Christianity, for a religion. He was making a claim about a person, Jesus Christ of Nazareth (Acts 4:10). Christianity is not the savior; Christ is. Much of what is called Christianity has not even begun to grasp who Jesus really is. Much of what is called Christianity has not even begun to realize the world-transforming consequences of Jesus' crucifixion and resurrection and subsequent exaltation as Lord. We are not claiming that Christianity is the one and only valid religion. We are claiming that Jesus Christ is the one and only Savior and Lord of the universe. He is the issue, the scandal of particularity.

We come back to the question: Why is there "no other name"? Why is salvation found in no one else? What do we say if a Hindu or Buddhist or Marxist asks us that question?

There are two basic answers to that question: There is no other name (1) because no one else said the things Jesus said; and (2) because no one else did the things that Jesus did.

Jesus' Words

No one else said the things Jesus of Nazareth said. For instance, no one has ever spoken with the authority with which he spoke. That is what struck his listeners after the Sermon on the Mount (Mt 7:28). Other teachers and prophets spoke *by* authority; Jesus spoke *with* authority.

Others introduced their prophecies with the solemn phrase, "Thus saith the Lord." Jesus said, "Truly, truly I say to you." Jesus even set his words in opposition to and over against the words of the religious authorities who came before him. Six times in the Sermon on the Mount he said, "You have heard that it was said . . . but I tell you . . . ." Who is this man who speaks with his own authority?

Also, no one else made himself the issue of his teaching the way Jesus did. He said, "Follow me," while others said follow the law, follow the way of love or follow the Eightfold Path to Enlightenment. Jesus said, "Follow me." Mohammed never made himself the issue of Islam. Buddha never made himself the issue of Buddhism. In fact, Buddha told his disciples that he could do nothing for them—they had to find their own way to enlightenment. A Jewish rabbi once observed that "no Moslem ever sings, 'Mohammed, lover of my soul,' nor does any Jew say of Moses, the Teacher, 'I need thee every hour.' " Jesus made himself the issue of his teachings—"Follow *me*," "Abide in *me*."

Furthermore, no one else made the kind of claims about himself that Jesus did: "I am the bread of life;" "I am the light of the world;" "I am the way and the truth and the life" (Jn 6:35; 8:12; 14:6). No one else, except Yahweh the God of the Hebrews, spoke like this.

Who is this man? Jesus did not simply claim to be a way, a truth, a life. He claimed to be the Way, the Truth, the Life. There is the scandal! Other teachers and prophets say, "Here is the path to life. Live in it." Jesus says, "I am the path. Live in me."

But Jesus said even more. Other teachers and prophets claimed to be sent by God; Jesus claimed to be sent from God. Other teachers claimed to represent God; Jesus claimed that in him God was actually present. He is God in human form. That claim was what generated the hostility of the leaders of Judaism. That claim got him crucified. In *God in the Dock* (Eerdmans), C. S. Lewis said it best: "If you had gone to Buddha and asked him 'Are you the son of Bramah?' he would have said, 'My son, you are still in the vale of illusion.' If you had gone to Socrates and asked, 'Are you Zeus?' he would have laughed at you. If you had gone to Mohammed and asked, 'Are you Allah?' he would first have rent his clothes and then cut your head off. If you had asked Confucius, 'Are you Heaven?,' I think he would have probably replied, 'Remarks which are not in accordance with nature are in bad taste.' "

When the Jews asked Jesus, "Who are you?" he answered, "Just what I have been claiming all along . . . before Abraham was born, I am" (Jn 8:25, 58). There is no other name because no one else said the things that Jesus said.

Jesus' Deeds

But there is a second reason that "salvation is found in no one else." *No one else did the things that Jesus did.* That is, no one else accomplished the kind of salvation Jesus Christ accomplished. No one else has even remotely claimed to do what Jesus claimed to be doing at the cross and through the empty tomb.

Every religious and philosophical system acknowledges that we human beings are caught in some sort of bondage. Jesus understood that bondage in a way no one else did. He saw us as hostages, held by the powers of sin, the demonic and death. And he saw that, try as we might, we cannot free ourselves. Other would-be saviors think we can free ourselves, and they offer steps to liberation. Jesus realized there are no steps out of the prison. So he came to do for us what we could not do for ourselves.

It was at the cross that he met the powers that keep us in bondage. It was at the cross that he fought the agonizing battle for us. For three days it appeared that death had won, that the darkness of death had finally snuffed out the Light of life. But on Easter morning Jesus broke out of the grave! Death had not won after all. He was alive! That fact makes Jesus different from all other saviors. In this man's life, death did not have the last word.

Death is the greatest enemy of life. The fear of death cripples us more than we realize. One could argue that all fear is ultimately rooted in the fear of death. And only Jesus can free us from that fear, for only Jesus has triumphed over death. Once he frees us from the fear of death, we are free to live. We are freed from the tyranny of grabbing for all the gusto because we know there is more to life than our few short years.

There is no other name in the universe by which we must be saved, because no one else said the things Jesus said and no one else did the things he did.

The scandal of particularity is posed by Jesus' own words and deeds. Once we face the fact that he, not we, caused the scandal, we are freed from our fears. Jesus Christ does not call us *to defend* him and his claims and deeds. He calls us to *proclaim* him and his claims and deeds. He can hold his own.

The Fish That Discovered Water: A Parable

by Harold Bredesen

Some scientists at Smolensk University decided to develop a fish that could live out of water.

So, choosing some healthy red herrings, they bred, crossbred, hormoned and chromosomed until at length they had a fish that could live—at least exist—out of water.

The local commissar was not satisfied. True, these fish had survived till now on rarefied gas, but how about reactionary tendencies? He suspected a secret yen for water.

"You have neglected education," he said. "Start over, and this time do not neglect education."

So again they bred, crossbred, hormoned and chromosomed, and this time they did not neglect education—down to the veriest reflex.

The result? A red herring that would rather die than get its tail wet. The slightest suggestion of humidity filled the new herring with dread. Thought control had done its perfect work, and, with the possible exception of the red herring, everyone was happy. Surely this year's Lenin Prize would go to the scientists of Smolensk University.

But the world must see this triumph of Soviet research, thought the commissar who had thought of education. So he took the fish on tour.

Somewhere in Hungary the tragedy occurred. Quite accidentally, according to official reports, the red herring fell into a pool of water.

Deep in the green translucent stuff it lay—eyes and gills clamped shut—afraid to move lest it become wetter. And, of course, it could not breathe—every reflex said no to that. Never did a fish so wet feel more like a fish out of water.

But breathe it must, and there was nothing else to breathe. Only water. So the red herring drew a tentative gillful.

Its eyes bulged. It breathed again. Its jaw flew open. It flicked a fin . . . then another . . . and wiggled with delight. Then it darted away. The fish had discovered water!

And with that same kind of wonder, men, conditioned by a world that rejects him, discover God. "For in him we live and move and have our being" (Acts 17:28).

How Do
We Do It?

Evangelistic Snapshot

I had encouraged Sue, a non-Christian, to read the Gospels herself and try to apply them to see if they had any relevance to her life. Several months later she told me her story:

"One day I read in the Bible, 'If someone steals your coat, don't let him have only that, but offer your cloak as well.' For whatever reason, that verse hit me between the eyes. So I said to the four walls, 'Listen walls—or God, if you're there—I'm going to do what this verse says, if the opportunity arises today. I'm doing this because I want to find out if Jesus really is who he says. Amen.'

"The day went by and I forgot the verse. Then I headed to the library to continue working on my senior thesis. Just as I sat at my designated thesis desk this guy comes up and starts yelling at me. He told me the school hadn't given him his thesis desk so he was going to take mine. I yelled back at him and pretty soon we caused quite a ruckus.

"Then it hit me.

"I just looked at him and moaned, 'Ohhhhhh, no. No. I can't believe it.' And to myself I thought, *Isn't there some other way* to find out if Jesus is God besides obeying that verse?

"But I couldn't escape the fact that I had read that verse the very same day someone tried to rob me. I took a deep breath, tried not to swear and said, 'Okay you can have the desk.'

"The guy was bewildered. As I headed out the door he grabbed my arm and asked why in the world I let him have it. I told him he would think I'd really flipped out, but I was trying to discover if Jesus was really who he claimed to be.

" 'Hey,' I continued, 'if there's one thing I've learned from reading about Jesus and meeting some real Christians, it's that Jesus would give you a lot more than a thesis desk if you'd let him. So that thesis desk is yours.'

"As I said those words, I just simply *knew* it was all true."
—Becky Pippert in *Out of the Saltshaker* (IVP).

Developing a Campus Strategy

by Andrew T. Le Peau

What's the key to effective evangelistic programs? After several frustrating years at the University of Denver, working hard at organizing Bible studies, prayer meetings, hayrides and booktables (and seeing meager results), I discovered what we had been doing wrong: our planning had been haphazard and our many different activities rarely fit with one another.

As a staff worker at Washington University I did two things differently. First, I realized that God had a specific vision for reaching the campus—a vision that we needed to discover. Second, we had to develop a well-thought-out plan for implementing it.

Here's how we and other groups have done it:

Ask God

We had overlooked the obvious. We needed to ask God. We had to learn not to rely on our own ideas and efforts and instead learn to come to God for direction. Jesus set the precedent when he said, "I do exactly what my Father has commanded me" (Jn 14:31). We first asked him to instill in us a desire for penetrating the major areas of our campus—geographically, academically and socially. We then prayed that he would show us his vision for our campus and that he guide us as we discussed how we were going to carry out this vision.

"Prayer walks" are a good way to do this. At Northwestern University, members of the campus fellowship would go out in groups of two at the beginning of the year and pray as they walked by dorms, Greek row, the library, the student center and the classrooms. They tried to pray about what they perceived to be the Holy Spirit's promptings rather than just praying from their own thoughts. After an hour everyone gathered together and compared notes. Invariably similar prayer concerns would emerge which would help develop a consensus of what dorms or student groups the fellowship should concentrate on that year. These "impressions," of course, would be verified as the group carried out the next steps listed here.

Identify Your School's "Personality"

Each campus fellowship is unique, and even more important, each campus is unique. What had been a smashing success at one school might bomb at another. To plot out our strategy we needed to research the makeup of our school and so we set out to answer the following questions:

☐ How many students are there and in what categories (grads, undergrads, majors)?

☐ Where are they located (dorms, frats, apartments)?

☐ What significant minorities are there?

☐ How many students have jobs?

☐ What is the campus mood or atmosphere (cold, friendly, apathetic)?

☐ What exerts an influence on students (the Greek system, Dr. Ruth Westheimer, the school newspaper)?

☐ How have things changed in the last few years (declining

enrollment, more faculty unrest, less social life)?

☐ What religious organizations are on campus, how big are they and what influence do they have?

Among many other things, our research revealed that our academically competitive and socially cold campus had five thousand grads who mostly lived off-campus and five thousand undergrads who lived mostly in dorms. By determining the campus' personality we were now ready to draw up a plan.

Develop a Strategy

In our brainstorming sessions we identified the strikingly different needs that grads and undergrads have. Assuming we had all the resources of time, people and money we needed, perhaps it would be best to have two different fellowships with two distinct programs, each meeting the particular needs of one of the primary groups. Yet both groups would probably focus on developing (1) an intellectual foundation for the Christian faith in the face of harsh skepticism; and (2) strong friendships that would stand in contrast to the campus' coldness.

Another campus fellowship had discovered that theirs was a "party" school of 17,000, made up of mostly undergrads living in dorms, where football and other social events were the only things that excited the whole campus. In their brainstorming sessions they decided to target the dorms for evangelistic outreach events and to sponsor buses to a nearby away game for anyone wanting to go. By plugging into the campus social scene in these and other ways, the members' deep commitment to Christ and one another, they theorized, would stand out in stark contrast to the superficiality of the rest of the campus.

The key is to mold the fellowship to the campus and not vice versa. This does not mean that we adopted the values or purposes of our campus, but that we, like Paul, "become all things to all men, so that by all means [we] might save some" (1 Cor 9:22). As we identified with our campus we were able to confront it at its point of need.

Determine Your Resources

After enjoying the luxury of pretending we had unlimited resources, we then returned to earth and practicalities. "Have two separate chapters? We barely have one, and only three or four grad students are involved!" someone exclaimed.

So we went back and looked at the questions we asked about our campus and asked them about our group. In addition we asked questions such as:

☐ What activities did the fellowship attempt last year and with what amount of success?

☐ How many students are core members and how many are on the fringe?

☐ Has the group been reaching out or reaching in? Why?

☐ What structural strengths and weaknesses does the fellowship have (solid network of small groups; the leaders do all the work; most of the members are seniors)?

Well, we only had three or four grad students. So we decided that these grads could start a grad Bible study with the goal that within three or four years it would develop into a good-sized group that would become the second fellowship.

At another school where ninety per cent of the chapter lived off-campus and ninety per cent of the campus lived in the dorms, things needed to change. They started with small steps like a few people volunteering to move back into the dorms. But they realized that a long-range plan would be necessary to bring things into the balance they wanted. Working up goals for where the chapter should be one, two and three years from now and concrete suggestions for getting there are essential for good long-term strategy.

These steps were only the beginning. As we immersed ourselves in them, God revealed other steps we needed to take. And this approach bore much more long-lasting and satisfying fruit.

God has a vision for your campus too. And he's anxious to show it to you.

Campus Evangelistic Events

*A*fter establishing your overall vision for reaching the campus, it's necessary to plan specific events and programs through which your evangelistic goals can be reached. On campuses throughout North America, students and campus fellowship staff have implemented effective programs. What follows are the wisdom and experiences of these people. The pieces are arranged in mostly chronological order, demonstrating the progression these activities should have.

Letter-Writing Campaign (by Dan Hamilton)
For years our fellowship never drew more than twenty-five or thirty members. Now we have about one hundred. The numbers started turning around when we started going out of our way to interact with incoming freshmen.

One year, when we were lamenting that we had lost several seniors to graduation and that the Greeks always seemed to nail newcomers before we could get to them, someone mentioned that the fraternities and sororities had access to a list of incoming freshmen. So why didn't we?

All we had to do was ask. When we approached the administration, they not only gave us the list but a pre-printed set of address labels. Next we got out some maps and marked the hometowns of our fellowship's members. Then we divided the incoming freshmen names by geographical area and assigned each willing fellowship member about twenty names from his or her area. One of the members prepared a flyer explaining the purpose of our group and ran off copies for all of us.

Over the summer, volunteers sent flyers and short personal notes to "their" freshmen. Then in the fall, though upperclassmen were not required to return until the week after freshmen, volunteers returned early to look up their contacts. And the chapter hosted a volleyball game and hot-dog roast on the first Saturday—the same time fraternities were hosting keg parties.

That first event was a hit. Many newcomers eventually became involved with the fellowship.

Our freshman-contact program grew. Each year more and more freshmen have become part of our fellowship because we reached out early and personally.

Daily Prayer Meetings (by Warren Starr)

It's not a new thought, but I believe it's true. The surest way to see growth in your campus fellowship is to sponsor daily times of corporate prayer.

Case in point: The University of Washington InterVarsity chapter, which held daily prayer meetings, was growing steadily and witnessing conversions. Then several students moved to another part of campus to start a ministry there. Their top priority was to begin a daily prayer meeting. A year later that campus fellowship had tripled in size and brought in ten new believers.

At the same time, the Central Washington University InterVarsity chapter was dying. One of two Bible studies fell apart.

No one came to Christ. I challenged the students at the Central chapter to commit themselves to praying together daily—even if it was only three of them. Central began having daily prayer meetings. A year later Central had placed thirty-six students in Bible studies and seen fourteen conversions!

The pattern seemed unmistakable. Everyone in both fellowships knew that God had honored the prayers of those in the daily prayer meetings.

Many works of God have begun with daily prayer meeting—including the student movement worldwide. The church itself was launched after the disciples had conducted a daily prayer meeting for forty straight days. And what results! Three thousand conversions in one day.

Evangelism, preaching and ministry to the poor that isn't undergirded with prayer leads to our attempting to do the work of God on campus without the power of God (see Mk 9:28-29). We become frustrated and burned out, or, if there is some success, proud.

Daily prayer meetings aren't a gimmick to make God work. They're just the opposite—an expression that we cannot manipulate God. Through prayer we humbly ask him to work in our midst because without him we can't do anything. Prayer meetings aren't a final step, either. The biblical model is to pray and act. Our experience at Central Washington University and the University of Washington has been that devoted prayer (which in itself is work) leads to action. Who knows what God will do on your campus if you gather daily to pray?

Here are some tips on how to get your group going:

Recruit daily prayer-meeting leaders as if you were recruiting chapter presidents. Although leading a prayer meeting generally doesn't take much time, it does require maturity. The leader should be respected, consistent and humble. (Graduate students make good candidates. Their schedules often keep them from other opportunities to lead and they can provide mature role models.)

Also enlist one or two people who will attend meetings every day. A few committed, enthusiastic people can move many to greater commitment.

Find a quiet location. Privacy helps participants relax and concentrate. Houses near campus, dorm rooms, or Christian houses on campus are good meeting places. Commuter students can reserve a room in the library or the student center.

The more comfortable the atmosphere the better. Having a carpet to sit on is best, but praying on a bare floor is often better than praying around a large table.

Keep meetings short; start and end on time. Thirty-minute meetings will easily work into a schedule. Constantly running late discourages people from coming. Good times to meet are a half-hour before classes begin in the morning, noon, right before dinner or late evening.

Here's a suggested schedule: The leader reviews yesterday's answers to prayer (some will probably be outrageous and fun) and asks for today's requests. This shouldn't take more than ten minutes. Then he or she reviews the list and leads off the prayer time by reading a worshipful psalm or song. Conversational prayer follows. With a minute left, the leader closes in prayer and the group sings a short song. And then it's off to class.

A schedule, rather than inhibiting people, frees them to pray effectively; unstructured prayer meetings usually degenerate into twenty-five minutes of gabbing and five minutes of shallow prayer.

I've found that there is no greater privilege and nothing more effective for campus evangelism than to come before the Father with our requests and for our instructions.

Media Blitz (by Thomas DeMeritt)

At our last campus fellowship meeting of the year, a stranger in the back raised his hand when I asked if anyone had announcements.

"Yes?" I nodded toward the hand. He stood up slowly and

cleared his throat. "I don't know exactly how to put this," he began. His earnestness commanded everyone's attention.

"I was a new Christian when I came to school here last fall. For weeks I looked for a Christian group similar to this one. Eventually I just forgot about it. This past year I've been doing a lot of things that a Christian shouldn't do. I'm sure this wouldn't have happened if I'd had a group of people like you to help me grow as a Christian. Can't you do something to let folks know you're here?"

We were shocked. We had no idea we were so cut off from the mainstream.

Unfortunately, that freshman's story is repeated every fall. Young Christians come to college looking for and needing Christian fellowship. Some who have difficulty finding it fall by the wayside.

Campus fellowships that make publicity a low priority pass up great opportunities for reaching out to new folks. Our group found out the hard way. But that next fall we found easy ways to become more visible. Here are some you can use on your campus.

☐ *Put fellowship activities on the school calendar.* Nearly every school puts one out, and nearly every student gets one. Typically, school calendars list games, holidays, fraternity and sorority happenings and so on. Get fellowship meetings listed and include the building, room and time. Meeting at the same time and place every week helps new students find you. If you don't have a regular meeting place, contact school officials *now* to get one for next fall.

☐ *Make your first meeting an event.* Kick off the year with something lighthearted: a bonfire, a picnic, a volleyball game. Mingle. Make welcoming newcomers (rather than reestablishing old friendships) your first priority. Toward the end have a good speaker briefly introduce your group and its goals; then announce the time, place and focus of the next meeting. Pass around a sign-up sheet, and personally invite each new person on your list to that next meeting.

☐ *Pursue official recognition.* Getting recognized by your school as a legitimate organization usually takes minimal effort and reaps great benefits, including listings in the school catalog and the yearbook.

☐ *Use campus radio and newspaper.* Most school radio stations will advertise campus meetings free. Make sure you provide them with enough information (who, what, where, when) and enough notice. Ditto with campus newspapers—providing them with a well-written report of special meetings, speakers, social functions and community projects can bring lots of exposure for little effort. Most papers carry a column of coming events. Make sure your meetings are included.

To help you out, InterVarsity has put together a complete publicity kit for campus groups, that includes info on working with editors, writing news releases, submitting photographs and writing announcements for radio. Send $4 for the *Chapter Publicity Kit* to 6400 Schroeder Rd., P.O. Box 7895, Madison WI 53707-7895.

☐ *Rush entering freshmen.* Freshmen who arrive on campus a few days before classes begin may feel disoriented, anxious to make new friends and eager for social invitations. Set up a table during registration (or whenever student groups set up displays for new students) and offer an easy-to-read sheet about your group.

☐ *Advertise meetings with inexpensive flyers.* Our school's printing department copied flyers for cost. Having folks from different dorms post catchy posters announcing meetings made for a quick and efficient PR network.

☐ *Create a big event.* Every year the campus looks forward to the annual "Watermelon-Seed-Spitting" contest sponsored by the Nassau Community College InterVarsity group.

According to staff worker Fran Thompson-Gee, running the contest, or any other similar event, is easy: On the count of three have the contestants attack their watermelon slices. The first to finish his or her piece without leaving any pink on the rind wins. Have the contestants save one watermelon seed in their mouths and then spit in turn. The one who spits it out the farthest wins. Pass out creative prizes.

During and after the contest give out free watermelon slices to spectators, and invite them to the group's first meeting. Hand them a colorful helium balloon with the date, time and place of the meeting, and a brochure (with the leaders' names and phone numbers) that describes the purposes and activities of your fellowship group.

Other similar events are a burger bash, a sundae party or a volleyball marathon.

Coffeehouse (by Steve Balkam)

I was tense. It was almost time to start and little seemed to be going according to plan. I had been racing up and down my dorm's stairs, frantically looking for lamps, extension cords and props. And Page was going over a skit for what sounded like the first time.

After praying together for a few minutes in the kitchen, I trotted out into a crowd of sixty impatient people. I jumped into my role as emcee.

"Hi, everybody, and thanks for coming to our coffeehouse. This is hosted by the Redlands Christian Fellowship, and it's something we'll be putting on every three weeks or so. Don't worry, we aren't going to preach at you or anything. We just want you to kick back, relax and enjoy yourselves."

And our show began.

As it turned out, I really shouldn't have worried so much at that first coffeehouse. It was a success. It fired us up and, after four years, the coffeehouse endures.

Setting up a coffeehouse is a lot of fun and it can be an effective way to make people think about spiritual issues. Here are some things we learned as we went along.

A coffeehouse will take different forms and names on different campuses. Though coffeehouses were big during the sixties, they are not an outmoded idea. A place where people can relax, have fun and be exposed to a fresh way of looking at life has always been popular on campuses. Coffeehouses can be replaced by a Coke lounge (Classic or New—take your pick!), a video night or take-time during finals week.

Whatever form your coffeehouse takes, it should primarily be a place where believers can bring friends who aren't familiar with Christianity. The coffeehouse's goal is to create a nonthreatening atmosphere that can expose the misconceptions believers and skeptics have of each other and, therefore, pave the way to friendships and to conversations about the meaning of life.

Gestures of care such as greeting people at the door, introducing guests to friends or serving a fancy snack help provide an environment of warmth and acceptance. The entertainment you dream up for the evening should be creative, funny and sensitive to the inquirers' frame of reference. Doing it this way will subtly open their eyes to perspectives they've never considered before. Try songs, magic shows, dance, skits. (Our Christian "rock video" was a great hit.) This is your chance to do your extraordinary dying-fish imitation for the Lord.

The coffeehouse also provided great leadership training. As people worked on it, the positive reinforcement they got gave them the courage to assume bigger responsibilities. As a freshman, Margene shared many bright ideas in brainstorming sessions, and so was asked to write a skit script for the first time. She grew from the chance to express Christ's message, instead of simply being on the receiving end.

Culinary artists in your group provide the greatest drawing card on campuses where the cafeteria can make many weep. A table with books, booklets or magazines that address some of the issues raised during the evening can also be set up.

The most important and rewarding result of the coffeehouse is that people come to know Christ. When Darrelle came to college, she was attending church once in a while, mostly out of obligation. But on our campus she heard the gospel in a way she could relate to.

"At the coffeehouse," Darrelle said, "I was glad there wasn't someone pointing a finger at me and saying, 'You're a sinner; you're doing wrong,' because a lot of people had said that to me before, and I would say, 'Who cares? It's my life, not yours.' The coffeehouse presents a message that leaves questions in your mind, and you can answer those questions yourself."

One skit Darrelle found especially thought-provoking featured two sheep who rebelled against a good and loving shepherd and struck out on their own. While some of us were amused with our sheep ears, Darrelle was laughing but at the same time thinking how rebellious she was being "to God, my parents and others." She began to realize that something was wrong with the way she was living. "Christians who befriended me at the coffeehouse and elsewhere on campus were really important to my becoming a Christian."

Dorm Talks (by Dietrich Gruen)

Coffeehouses and watermelon-seed-spitting contests are good ways to make friends with non-Christians while at the same time sharing the love of Christ with them. You should also think about creating opportunities to present the gospel to them directly. Organizing a discussion on Jesus' claims with your non-Christian friends in your dorm, fraternity, sorority or apartment building is an excellent way to do this.

There are many different approaches to staging a dorm talk, and what follows are a few ways you can do it. But the bottom line with each of these ideas is to let your friends know what the gospel is and to stimulate discussion about it.

☐ Distribute an IVP booklet (such as *What Is Christianity?* or *Can I Believe Christianity?*) to everyone who lives on a dorm floor. As you do so, invite people to read the booklet and come to the dorm lounge two nights later for a group discussion about the issues raised in the booklet.

□ Show a movie that raises faith and lifestyle issues, and follow it up with an organized discussion afterward.

□ Invite a campus-oriented speaker (your staff worker or faculty adviser, for example) to come in and give a Christian testimony or biblical perspective on some of the current issues students are up against. Residence hall advisers will even sponsor such events to fulfill part of their quota of "cultural" activities in their dorms.

It's important to know your audience before you decide on the approach you're going to take. Is your living unit composed of mostly semi-alcoholic party types? You might want to schedule your gospel discussion around the weekly dorm keg party. Raise the question (in normal conversation and in public posters), "What If Jesus Christ Came to a Dorm Keg Party?" One group even sponsored a Beer 'n' Bible Nite.

Suppose mostly nose-in-the-books types live in your dorm. Then you would want to pitch your gospel discussion accordingly: "Does Becoming a Christian Mean Intellectual Suicide?" Is your living unit mostly made up of socially conscious students? Then perhaps a presentation on Jesus' view of wealth and poverty or racism would be effective. All-male, jock-type fraternities would more likely listen to and respect a Christian athlete than a college professor.

Since dorm talks usually are not a time to harvest but a time to sow, follow-up is a must. Order Bibles, study guides and other literature for new Christians and interested seekers to use afterward. After the discussion, announce that anyone interested can participate in a three- or four-week Bible study that would meet at a time convenient for them. (Make sure that you have lined up people beforehand who would be willing to lead investigative Bible studies or do one-on-one follow-up.)

Having a handout that people can fill out after the meeting will facilitate this follow-up. The handout should summarize the salient points of the message presented plus contain a tear-off response form where people can write down their impressions or indicate their desire to pursue the subject more.

One final caution: No matter how on-target your advertising pitch or how timely your scheduling, non-Christians will not come to Christian-sponsored events unless you really have friends on your dorm floor with whom you have done things regularly. Maybe you need to go with your friends to their thing before inviting them to yours.

Investigative Bible Studies (by Betsy Rossen Elliot)

Dorm talks are one good way to launch investigative Bible studies. But there are other ways as well.

During my junior year in college, my roommate, Barb, and I had a remarkable camaraderie with the other women in our dorm that grew into just such an investigative study. Here are some principles we learned.

☐ *Reach out with a friend.* There are times and places to be a lone voice crying in the wilderness. An investigative study in your dorm or neighborhood is not one of them. It's great to share the joys and the problems with a Christian friend, someone with whom you can plan and pray.

It also gives the people in your study a chance to see the varieties of religious faith and to see that they don't have to be or act a certain way (namely, a clone of you) to seriously consider the claims of Christ.

☐ *Talk and dream.* Barb and I had spent the first semester building our own friendship as well as reaching out to others on our corridor. And as we talked before the second semester began, it seemed that forming a group study was worth considering.

We agreed almost immediately on whom God seemed to be leading us to invite—they included Diane, who needed some encouragement to rekindle her childhood faith; her roommate, Lynn, who challenged, yet seemed curious about, our religious beliefs; and Sara, who joked about being overweight but indirectly asked questions about whether God loved her. If you have these kinds of relationships on campus, you'll realize as we did, how much genuine friendship and openness are already there.

☐ *Invite people to investigate.* Sharing your love for Jesus can be the natural next step to take. We invited them to the study during the first week of the semester, and nearly everyone accepted eagerly. When you talk with people, don't be defensive about introducing Christ and his claims. But don't be pushy either, and respect the fact that the group setting, timing or other factors might make it difficult for someone to accept the invitation. Be sure not to make anyone feel like a second-class citizen for turning you down; don't offer conditional friendship.

☐ *Choose a good study guide.* It's always possible to make up your own discussion questions as you go, but a carefully chosen guidebook can free you from many hours of preparation and will help you make sure that the friendships (and your studies) don't get pushed aside.

Many fine study guides are available. Choose one that's appropriate in tone, topic and time commitment for your group. We decided on an eight-week study of the Gospel of John, using the IVP study guide *Jesus the Life Changer* by Ada Lum. The study began during the second week of classes.

☐ *Keep being a friend.* We were glad that our study became a normal part of the week, not an awkward shifting of gears that communicates, "Now it's time to act religious." Be understanding about fluctuations in attendance—exams and papers press in on even the best-intentioned.

Avoid the trap of being the perfectly pious one now that you're leading a Bible study. You don't have to have all the answers during your discussion time. Be yourself and be open to your friends and to God. For us, being ourselves meant continuing our comedy routines at dorm functions and putting a sign on our door offering writing and math help.

☐ *Be faithful and leave the results to God.* The success of your study will not be measured by lightning-bolt conversions or the startling sermons that you preach during the studies. In fact, a sure sign of a failing study is if you find yourself talking too much. Instead, enjoy opening yourself to your friends and reinvestigating Jesus' claims with them.

What happened in our study? Nothing earthshaking, but Diane renewed her faith and became active in our campus fellowship. And all of them expressed appreciation for what they'd learned in the Bible and what they'd seen in Barb's and my friendship for each other and for them. (Meanwhile, bookings for our comedy routine increased sharply.) We're pretty sure that God will use those hours of study in the years to come. What might God have in store for you and your friends this term?

Bringing the Gospel to Fraternity Row

by Edward Focht

I have no doubt that if Jesus were to visit a college campus today he would hang out on Greek Row. During his ministry on earth Jesus often went out of his way to be at the parties and homes of the most hedonistic people in his society. No wonder they accused him of being a glutton and a drunkard (Lk 7:34).

When I joined Theta Chi, I had no idea what to expect. I was a Christian and eager to share my faith, but I wasn't sure how to go about it in the frat house.

After a few months I noticed a few things. The first was that my fraternity brothers were not that much different than me. I had as many doubts, fears and hurts as they did—the difference being that I was learning to find solace and peace in the Lord while they were trying to find the same in relationships, owning things, doing drugs or drinking.

The second and most important thing I noticed was that joining a fraternity (or sorority) to share Christ with others would mean personal sacrifice in many different areas.

Probably my most difficult sacrifice was taking ridicule from my fraternity brothers when I opened up about my faith. God, however, helped me to not give up. Slowly, as I prayed consistently and lived a life of integrity, the ridicule of the first year turned into respect.

I also noticed that the more time I spent with my frat brothers, the more effect I had; so making friendships in the house became a top priority. This led to another sacrifice: choosing not to pursue and develop a deep involvement with a girlfriend so that I could spend quality time with the brothers. Of course, living in the same house with them did not automatically translate into quality relationships—I had to work at them.

Saying good-by to my privacy and comfort was another sacrifice. Often discussions or counseling sessions would arise late at night when I would have preferred to sleep. I maintained an open-door policy so anyone could enter whenever he wished. I could have remained more isolated, but that would have deterred the openness vital for seeing God's kingdom grow.

As my personal sacrifices increased, growth and effectiveness in spreading God's kingdom also increased. Jesus' words in Luke 9:23 became real to me: "If anyone would come after me, he must deny himself and take up his cross daily and follow me." The scalpel of sacrifice slices away all the extras of the world so that we can wholeheartedly enjoy life with and for him.

Investment Returns

Prayer proved my most effective activity. It didn't come easy though. I almost let my activities as president of the InterVarsity chapter justify my lack of intercession for both Christians and non-Christians. A character study on Moses one year impressed on me the importance of concentrated prayer and fasting. Twice Moses, while he was responsible for over a million Israelites, extricated himself from his busy routine to be with God for forty straight days and nights. I found myself hard pressed to barely set aside one hour a week on Sunday to pray for my frat brothers. But I'm glad I did.

During those prayer times God consistently worked on draining the pride in my heart and filling it with a greater love for my friends. I learned to empathize with them instead of judging them because of their sins. The result? Increased communication and openness with my brothers which increased God's presence at Theta Chi. If only I had grasped these principles sooner!

Establishing good relationships paved the way for more planned evangelistic events. One night, after another campus fellowship team gave their testimonies after dinner, two brothers made decisions for Christ. This was only a warm-up for what was to come.

During my senior year I cultivated the field with Bible studies, times of prayer and fasting and one-on-one conversations as other Christians were led to join the fraternity. Then, at one of our last major functions of the year, the brothers allowed me to give a challenging speech centered on accepting Jesus as Savior and Lord. I wasn't prepared for the response—fifteen of the forty brothers stood to either commit or recommit their lives to Christ.

How About You?
How can you know whether God is leading you into a fraternity or sorority where you would grow not only in character but also as a useful channel of God?

First consider your strength and weaknesses. Do you have a weakness for alcohol? If so, joining a frat will only play on that weakness. Is your relationship with God strong? Fraternity lifestyles and values will constantly create dilemmas for you which only spiritual discernment and godly wisdom can help resolve.

Consider joining with another Christian. Jesus sent the disciples out two by two; so when one fell or became discouraged, the other was available for support and encouragement, both in word and in prayer. A fraternity or sorority is no exception.

One last word about the pressure of Greek Rush. Do not be swayed by the glib tongue of a Greek to join prematurely. You should establish relationships with members of at least three houses before you pledge. Tactfully share your beliefs and motivation for joining as God leads. If you are a freshman, pledge during your sophomore year. If you are a sophomore, wait until spring. You will be pressured to be quantity-time oriented instead of quality-time oriented from the start. Stand your ground, and do not let your priorities become confused. Remember, getting to know God is first, studies come second, and Greek involvement is third.

Even for those who feel strong and led by God to join a Greek house, it is a morally dangerous decision. But if you are truly strong in your relationship with Jesus and motivated to serve him, guided by God's Holy Spirit, he will take those dangerous situations and develop them into stretching experiences that will bring glory to God.

Paul preached to the Greeks. So can you!

How Not to Witness to Your Non-Christian Prof

by Billy Fong

I envied Thomas, a bright student in my sociology of religion course. He was a double major in history and philosophy, and with his grasp of key figures and movements, he seemed to conduct a private conversation with the prof during each class. I would've liked to have engaged the professor in conversation too. But as a Christian I was sure my ideas on religion would be shot down.

Later in the term I ran into Thomas at a Christian concert. "Are you a Christian?" I asked, surprised.

"Yes, I am," he replied, wondering why I'd even raise the question.

"Oh, I didn't know that," I continued.

"Why? Doesn't my conduct in class seem like it?" he asked a bit defensively.

Assuring him I didn't intend to imply that, I walked away from the encounter with a new understanding of how Christians could relate to their professors.

Escaping the Lion's Den

It had been comforting to see myself as Daniel in the lions' den when it came to classes that discussed religion. But after talking with Thomas I realized that instead of reacting defensively to negative statements professors made of Christianity, my interactions with professors could be constructive if I earned the right to be heard.

The first step in doing this was to understand what was being taught before I launched into criticism. After all, hearing and understanding what a professor was teaching did not mean I had to embrace all its implications and compromise my faith. Rejecting presuppositions without knowing what they are, simply was not fair nor responsible.

Finding out where professors were coming from was a way to gain their trust. In that same sociology of religion course, for example, my professor openly admitted his liberal theological orientation the first day of class. Later in the term, as I worked on getting to know him more personally, I discovered he had grown up in an evangelical tradition quite similar to mine. In seminary, as a result of a few obscure, and perhaps misconstrued, comments from one prominent evangelical pastor and another noted evangelical scholar, he had embraced a liberal universalism (that is, he thought everyone would be saved eventually). Finding out about my professor's spiritual journey helped me to understand him better—and my interest in him as a person built mutual respect between us.

So later in the semester I recommended he read *Dynamics of Spiritual Life* by Richard Lovelace (IVP), a book that pointed out how the agendas of liberalism and evangelicalism (in areas such as social concern) seem to be coming back together again. By taking into account his intellectual pilgrimage, I could talk with him about faith issues more effectively.

It's Not All Academic

Not all professors were so open or congenial, however. And

neither were their antagonisms toward Christianity solely due to intellectual reasons. Profs, like many others, have often had hurtful personal experiences that color their view of Christianity.

Once, as I was trying to clarify a statement I'd written in a paper regarding the church, my history professor brashly retorted that I did not need to enlighten him since he had grown up in the church—and away from it. "In addition," he said resentfully, "I fought for years to get a history course on the Bible taught in a secular university, only to have numerous church groups fight me all the way." Under other circumstances, my professor's response would have been strictly academic, but I had struck a nerve. I needed to respond sensitively to his deep and bitter wounds.

Most professors are open to intellectual challenges; that's why they've chosen the academic world. But they are also people with hurts, dreams and experiences that require that we extend to them the grace and mercy of God.

Every year professors influence the thinking of hundreds, if not thousands, of students. But that doesn't mean they can't be influenced themselves. And if they are influenced in God's direction, the ripple effect will be immeasurable.

Reaching Out to International Students

by Jane Hopson and Andrés Tapia

I*n Europe people get along with you very easily, but this is not* true in the U.S.," says a Palestinian student studying in Illinois. "That's why we internationals feel so isolated. In class people are social, but outside of class nobody seems to care. It really hurts."

The World at Our Doorstep
This student echoes the complaint of many of the nearly 500,000 international students at U.S. and Canadian colleges and universities. The fast pace of campus life, along with financial difficulties (often due to unfavorable currency rates) and homesickness, adds to the tension of being in an alien cultural setting and having to operate in a foreign language.

Though you usually see them hanging out with other internationals, they are usually frustrated they don't spend more time with North Americans. After all, that's one of the reasons they came. Many internationals return to their country never having entered a North American home, and with few *gringo* names in their address books.

Christians—because of their historical concern for the alien in their midst and their commitment to sharing the gospel to the ends of the earth—are among the best qualified to meet the needs of those students under the turbans, ponchos and saris.

Tips for Crossing the Cultural Gap

Here are some tips on building friendships with internationals that you may find helpful:

□ Don't be afraid to take the initiative in establishing a relationship with an international student. Since they are often unsure about how things work and how one is supposed to behave in our culture, they are usually very open and appreciative when someone takes the time to befriend them.

□ Ask questions about a person's culture and country. Since internationals miss their countries so much, they are eager to talk about them.

□ Read about other parts of the world in your daily newspaper or weekly news magazine. Knowing about current events in an international's country can help open up conversations (you'll probably find that your friend knows more about international—and even North American—politics than you do).

□ Keep your eye open for things that seem new to them and then offer to help. Many of these will be things you take for granted—using the library, taking the bus, ordering fast food at a drive-thru, using a laundromat, shopping for sales, opening up a checking account.

□ Take them to events or places typically North American: Christmas caroling, a Fourth of July BBQ picnic, a pro football or ice hockey game, an automated car wash, a shopping mall.

□ Take them to your home so they can see how a North American family lives or to family events such as a wedding, a baptism or Thanksgiving dinner. Or simply do routine things such as studying together.

☐ Pray often for your international friends. Most internationals, especially those from countries closed to missionaries, are curious about Christianity. Conversations about your faith will emerge naturally as your friendship develops, but don't make your friendship contingent on them becoming Christians.

A few cautions: let your motivation be a desire for friendship and welcoming someone to your country instead of a duty done out of obligation or to score some spiritual points; and due to different cultural assumptions and norms, it's usually better, at least initially, to befriend someone of the same sex.

For a bibliography of resources on international students, write: Ned Hale, International Student Ministry, InterVarsity Christian Fellowship, 6400 Schroeder Rd., P.O. Box 7895, Madison, WI 53707-7895.

Facing Your Family: How One Student Almost Blew It

by Tom L. Eisenman

O ne evening, *about two weeks before Christmas, I heard a* knock at the back door of the small house I was renting. When I opened it, my dad was there, banging the heavy Wisconsin snow off his boots. He came in, sat down at the table, and told me he had a very hard thing to say.

"We don't want you to come home this Christmas," he said quietly. He couldn't even look me in the eyes as he spoke. "If you're there, you'll just spoil things for the rest of us."

I was shocked. My dad is one of the most loving, gentle men I've ever known, and our family has always been very close. So something dreadful had to be happening for him to tell me that I wasn't welcome home for Christmas.

On Becoming a Christian Monster

Dad's bomb opened my eyes to something I didn't want to see. Ever since I had become a Christian two months earlier, I had been alienating my entire family. After Dad left, and during the next few days, I reflected on how poorly I had demonstrated to my family the newfound love I claimed.

As a new Christian relating to non-Christian parents, I made every mistake in the book. For openers, I thought my family members needed to know that they were all going to hell. (I told them that for their own good, of course!) After clarifying that issue, I let them know that I couldn't hang around them anymore because their bad influence might rub off on me. So I hardly went home at all, spending all my time with my new Christian friends. When I did drop in, it was usually with some ulterior motive, such as letting them know that their celebrating Jesus' birthday with a lot of drinking and gluttony was sinful.

The contrast between how I related to my family before becoming a Christian and now couldn't have been greater. We had always gotten along great, but now as a Christian I was telling them in no uncertain terms that their lives—and the twenty years of effort and sacrifice they had poured into me—amounted to nothing. On top of that, most of the activities we had enjoyed together as a family suddenly showed up on my long list of mortal sins. My behavior was speaking more loudly than my words.

As I put myself in their shoes, I began to better understand my parents' attitudes toward my conversion. Why should I expect my mom and dad to support something that appeared to be splitting our family and stealing their son away? They had heard so much about cults. My behavior suggested all of the worst things to them. Being a witness should have meant spending *more* time at home than ever before, and serving and caring for them more sacrificially.

And why shouldn't they be skeptical about my new decision and lifestyle? After all, they knew me better than anyone else and had seen me go through an Eastern religion phase, a TM phase, a flirtation with psychedelic drugs—and now I was a Christian. To them it looked exactly like just one more crazy detour in my life. My parents would need to see positive changes in me over a long period of time before I could expect them to consider believing in Christ themselves.

I also realized I had unrealistic expectations of my parents' ability to change. As a student it was relatively easy for me to alter my life's patterns, but older adults are different. Their lives are full of long-term patterns not easily broken. I had to learn to slow down and trust God more.

It helped to remember that *I was not ultimately responsible for my parents' faith.*

What finally put my obnoxious behavior in perspective was seeing the stark contrast between how I presented my faith to my friends and how I presented it to my family. While I listened patiently to my friends' points of view, I would get very impatient with Mom and Dad. In addition, my most heated arguments were over topics that made little or no difference a week or even a day later. Why did I waste so much energy over relatively unimportant things? I saw that the quality of my relationship with my parents had to be my "evangelistic priority."

Remembering to Love

After these reflections I knew what I needed to do. A few days after my dad's visit, I did the first loving thing since becoming a Christian that October. I asked my whole family to forgive me for being so arrogant, judgmental and obnoxious. We shared some tears together. It was the beginning of a new relationship that became deeper and better than I would've ever dreamed possible. I was welcomed home for Christmas after all.

One trip home later in the new year exemplified our renewed relationships. While Dad and I were driving out to the grocery store on a Saturday morning, he told me that the company he worked for had moved to a new building. I asked him where his new plant was located—and if we could stop by so I could see his office. You wouldn't believe how excited he was that I would care at all about what he did Monday through Friday every week. The hour I took to tour the plant with him was the highlight for him (and for me!) of my visit home.

I had come to believe in Jesus' love for me as I saw his great interest in who I was and what I did. I had finally realized I could do no less for my parents.

Facing Your Parents: Practical Tips

by Ward Patterson

T*he following guidelines can help you to avoid making the* common mistakes new Christians make with their parents—or, if you already have stuck both feet in your mouth, these tips will help you get them out:

Pray your head off for your parents. This step will help you do the others. It is in prayer that God confronts us about our own sinful attitudes and, through the process of repentence and forgiveness, prepares us to represent Christ to our parents.

Also try praying with others about non-Christian parents— it's good to know you're not alone. Once, when a student phoned her parents during a particularly difficult confrontation, other students in the next room were praying for the call. After she hung up, she joyfully told her praying friends about the first conversation she had had with her parents in months that had not ended in angry tears.

Create an atmosphere of trust. Talking about your faith will come naturally as you communicate openly with your parents about all areas of your life, and as you confide in them your fears and struggles.

Also, consider asking forgiveness—even if you weren't the only one at fault—for the times when you lashed out, stomped out, sulked or otherwise punished your parents. It will go a long way in breaking down past barriers.

Be sensitive to your parents' beliefs and concerns. Have you ever talked with your parents about personal faith before? If not, then first try to discern what their understanding of the Christian faith is. Let them articulate their beliefs in their own way—something they might be doing for the first time.

Listen not only to what your parents are saying, but also to what is behind what they are saying. "We want you to be careful not to get tied up with some strange religious group" might be a legitimate and sincere concern for your good.

And sharing with your parents the process by which you came to faith, and not just the result of the process, will help them see that your conversion has been thoughtfully and seriously undertaken rather than sudden and capricious.

Put yourself in their shoes. For eighteen years or more your parents have been the voice of wisdom and experience in your life. To say that Christ has become that reference point can be very threatening. Assure them that their importance in your life has not diminished.

It can also be difficult for them to accept that their son or daughter might well be able to teach them something of lasting importance. Be sensitive to how you are coming across to them—a patronizing or holier-than-thou attitude will undermine your witness.

Let your deeds do the speaking. Remember their birthdays and anniversaries. Remember their likes and dislikes and surprise them now and then. Write often, even if briefly. Parents value letters more than students know.

Ask yourself: Do I take it for granted that my parents owe me a college education? Do I ever express appreciation for the sacrifices they make for me? Do I do my best to wisely use the money I receive from them? Do I look for ways to relieve them of the burden of looking after my material needs, or do I exploit their generosity?

Anticipate their skepticism—and ride it out. Your parents may test the strength of your faith against their criticism and belittlement to see how soon they can get you to return to your old patterns. They want to see just what your faith is made of. (Why shouldn't they?) If, in love, your faith withstands and flourishes, it will be a more powerful witness to them.

Be warned that even if you follow these guidelines, your parents might still choose to interpret your faith as a rejection of them. This is why you must take pains to convey love in as many ways as possible without compromising your faith—and leave the rest to God.

Encouraging a Decision

by Paul Little

So *what do you do now? You have established good, genuine* relationships with your roommates, classmates, parents and profs—you have even had fruitful discussions with them about your faith. But they still have not made a decision about receiving Jesus. How will you be able to tell when your friend is ready to accept Christ?

The answer, actually, is quite simple—ask.

Over the years I've used a couple of very simple questions to find out where people stand. "Have you ever personally trusted Christ or are you still on the way?" worked almost every time. This sufficiently described a Christian so that the average person did not say yes unless he or she knew what I meant. If the person didn't understand the question, I could deduce that he or she wasn't a believer and it quite naturally gave me the opportunity to explain the gospel.

Most, however, would respond, "That's me, I'm still on the way." Then I would ask my second question, "How far along the way are you?" Without inhibition or embarrassment the person usually told me.

Talking It Through

Important or trivial objections to becoming a Christian often popped up at this time. Some complained that they didn't know enough. I would point out that it was not a question of how much they knew, but whether they believed and were ready to respond to what they did know. "A person never fully understands the gospel," I would say. "If we wait until we fully understand, we will never trust Christ."

Sometimes a person would object, "But I'm not good enough." I liked answering this because I could help my friend see that this was exactly the kind of person for whom Christ died.

Others were concerned: "I don't think I could last and I don't want to be a hypocrite." My answer? "It's not a question of holding on to Christ and hoping that your grip will not fail. Rather, Christ grasps hold of you. In John 10:28, Jesus has said that he gives his sheep eternal life, they shall never perish and no one can pluck them out of his hand."

As I shared with my friends I learned to avoid two extremes—precipitation and procrastination. The first, pushing people into a decision they were not prepared for, not only was wrong but usually backfired. The second, letting them put the decision off as though it were not important, undermined my message that the issue was a matter of life and death that demanded a response.

When Sergio indicated that he wanted to receive Christ, I explained that to become a Christian there was something to be believed and someone to be received. Christ's deity, life, death and resurrection, and his diagnosis of our sinful condition are the essence of the Christian faith. But mere intellectual assent to those facts does not make a person a Christian. He must receive Christ into his life and become a child of God.

Sergio had trouble with this concept so I compared it to marriage. "Belief in the other person does not make us married. We must respond with our will in order to establish a relationship. In becoming a Christian we believe in Jesus and then receive him into our lives. Only then can we say we have a relationship with God." John 1:12 explains this.

I would also use Revelation 3:20 to help a person understand the need to invite Jesus into his or her heart. "Suppose someone came to the door of your home and knocked. How would you let the knocking person inside?" I asked Jackie. She thought for a moment and said, "I would open the door." After agreeing with that, I said, "And then what would you do?" A smile broke across her face as she said, "I would invite the person to come in." "This is exactly how you become a Christian," I told her. "Christ is knocking at the door of your life. He wants to come in to become the Lord of your life, but he will never force his way in or gatecrash. Instead, the moment you invite him to come in, he will." Before praying with her I asked Jackie to explain it back to me. As she repeated the essence of what I had told her, I knew she had heard and understood correctly.

Prayer
Once the person definitely wanted to receive Christ and seemed to understand what was involved, I would suggest several options about praying to receive Christ. If he or she wasn't accustomed to praying, I would offer to pray a prayer which could be repeated after me phrase by phrase. After saying what my prayer would include, I emphasized the fact that the words themselves had no magic. Unless they represented what my friend really felt in his or her heart, they did not mean anything.

Gabriel preferred to pray silently, and I offered him that option. Then, after he had prayed silently and I had prayed audibly, I asked him what he had said to God. He, like many others, had thanked God for the birds and his friends and the sunset. I then asked him if he had really spoken to Jesus Christ and thanked him for dying for his sins and invited him into his life as Lord and master. "I guess not," he answered. So I suggested he pray again, addressing himself to the Lord in those terms.

Others, on the other hand, preferred to go back to their rooms to pray. If they did, I urged them to call me or see me within twenty-four hours to tell me the decision they had made.

After the prayer of conversion some people would feel tremendously relieved. Others had little feeling at all. This varied with the individual. I made sure they knew that the assurance of salvation rested on what Christ had done on the cross and that it did not depend on how they felt at the moment.

Follow-up

I soon realized that my work was not over once the person had accepted Christ. Good follow-up is crucial. New Christians need help to begin reading the Word of God for themselves. I usually suggested a specific passage, such as the beginning of the Gospel of Mark. Giving them questions to ask themselves about the text also proved helpful (such as "What does this teach me about Christ?" or "Is there a command I should obey or an example to follow?").

New Christians also need help in their relationships with non-Christian friends and family. I would see new Christians alienate their families due to their misdirected zeal. To tell family members they don't know the gospel often makes them resentful. If the person came from a nominally Christian family, I suggested it would be more constructive to assume his or her family understood the facts of the gospel, and to tell them so. Then he or she could simply say that these facts had suddenly become alive and meaningful in his or her life and that's why it was important to share with them what had happened.

I would suggest breaking from non-Christian friends only if

I saw that they were going to sweep the new Christian into an old life of sin. New Christians usually have more contacts with non-Christians than Christians do, making them excellent evangelists—especially as their friends see how knowing Jesus is changing the new Christian.

Scripture teaches us that God wants to use us in reaping as well as in sowing and watering. Many more of us would have the privilege of being the last link in the chain if we "popped the question" to more people than we do. Take time right now to think about your circle of friends. Is there someone who is waiting to be asked? If you were to approach that person in love, you might be able to help him or her make a specific decision for Christ. Few things are more precious.

Acknowledgments

The chapter "Why I'm Not a Christian: A Report" by Robert M. Kachur was originally published in HIS magazine, February 1986. Copyright © 1986 Robert M. Kachur. Used by permission.

The chapter "I Saw Gooley Fly: A Parable" by Joseph T. Bayly was originally published as "I Saw Gooley Fly" in HIS magazine, 1954. Copyright © 1954 Joseph T. Bayly. Used by permission.

The chapter "What It Is and What It Isn't" by Terrell Smith was originally published as "How to Develop an Evangelistic Lifestyle" in *HIS Guide to Evangelism* (Downers Grove, Ill.: InterVarsity Press, 1977). Copyright © 1977 InterVarsity Christian Fellowship of the USA. Used by permission.

The chapter "Jesus' Style: Delightful and Disturbing" by Rebecca Manley Pippert was originally published as "Jesus: Delightful & Disturbing" in HIS magazine, May 1979. Copyright © 1979 Rebecca Manley Pippert. Used by permission.

The chapter "Four Roads to Faith" by Samuel Escobar was originally published in HIS magazine, March 1979. Copyright © 1979 Samuel Escobar. Used by permission.

The chapter "The Search for Truth" by Rich Lang was originally published as "A Ring of Truth" in HIS magazine, December 1983. Copyright © 1983 Rich Lang. Used by permission.

The chapter "Meeting Jesus through Friendships" by Paul Tokunaga was originally published as "Gary Became My Friend" in HIS magazine, December 1985. Copyright © 1985 Paul Tokunaga. Used by permission.

The chapter "Campus Casualty: A Parable" by C. Stephen Board was originally published as "Campus Casualty: A Case Study" in *HIS Guide to Evangelism* (Downers Grove, Ill.: InterVarsity Press, 1977). Copyright © 1977 InterVarsity Christian Fellowship of the USA. Used by permission.

The chapter "Is Jesus God? An Otherworldly Debate" by Peter Kreeft was adapted from *Between Heaven and Hell* (Downers Grove, Ill.: InterVarsity Press, 1982). Copyright © 1982 InterVarsity Christian Fellowship of the USA. Used by permission.

The chapter "Is Jesus the Only Way?" by Darrell W. Johnson was originally published as "There Is No Other Name: The Scandal of Particularity" in HIS magazine, December 1984. Copyright © 1984 Darrell W. Johnson. Used by permission.

The chapter "The Fish That Discovered Water: A Parable" by Harald Bredesen was originally published as "The Fish That Discovered Water" in HIS magazine, April 1976. Copyright © 1976 Harald Bredesen. Used by permission.

The chapter "Developing a Campus Strategy" by Andrew T. LePeau was originally published as "Spying Out the Land" in *HIS Guide to Evangelism* (Downers Grove, Ill.: InterVarsity Press, 1977). Copyright © 1977 InterVarsity Christian Fellowship of the USA. Used by permission.

The chapter "Letter-Writing Campaign" by Dan Hamilton was originally published in HIS magazine, April/May 1986. Copyright © 1986 Dan Hamilton. Used by permission.

The chapter "Daily Prayer Meetings" by Warren Starr was originally published as "Daily Prayer Meetings: Worth the Hassle?" in HIS magazine, October 1985. Copyright © 1985 Warren Starr. Used by permission.

The chapter "Media Blitz" by Thomas E. DeMeritt was originally published in HIS magazine, April/May 1986. Copyright © 1986 Thomas E. DeMeritt. Used by permission.

The chapter "Coffeehouse" by Steve Balkam was originally published as "Launching a Coffeehouse on Your Campus" in HIS magazine, December 1985. Copyright © 1985 Steve Balkam. Used by permission.

The chapter "Dorm Talks" by Dietrich Gruen was originally published as "Setting Up a 'Dorm Talk' " in HIS magazine, December 1983. Copyright © 1983 Dietrich Gruen. Used by permission.

The chapter "Investigative Bible Studies" by Betsy Rossen Elliot was originally published as "Launching an Evangelistic Bible Study" in U magazine, January 1987. Copyright © 1987. Used by permission.

The chapter "Bringing the Gospel to Fraternity Row" by Edward Focht was originally published as "Translating the Gospel into Greek" in *HIS Guide to Evangelism* (Downers Grove, Ill.: InterVarsity Press, 1977). Copyright © 1977 InterVarsity Christian Fellowship of the USA. Used by permission.

The chapter "How Not to Witness to Your Non-Christian Prof" by Billy Fong was originally published in HIS magazine, December 1983. Copyright © 1983 Billy Fong. Used by permission.

The chapter "Reaching Out to International Students" by Jane Hopson and Andrés Tapia was originally published in "The World on Your Campus" in U magazine, February 1987. Copyright © 1987 Jane Hopson and Andrés Tapia. Used by permission.

The chapter "Facing Your Family: How One Student Almost Blew It" by Tom L. Eisenman was originally published as "Going Home for Christmas" in HIS magazine, December 1983. Copyright © 1983 Tom L. Eisenman. Used by permission.

The chapter "Facing Your Parents: Practical Tips" by Ward Patterson was originally published as "Facing Your Parents for the First Time" in HIS magazine, December 1978. Copyright © 1978. Used by permission.

The chapter "Encouraging a Decision" by Paul E. Little was originally published in *HIS Guide to Evangelism* (Downers Grove, Ill.: InterVarsity Press, 1977). Copyright © 1977 InterVarsity Christian Fellowship of the USA. Used by permission.

The "Evangelistic Snapshots" are taken from *Out of the Saltshaker* by Rebecca Manley Pippert (Downers Grove, Ill.: InterVarsity Press, 1979); copyright © 1979 InterVarsity Christian Fellowship of the USA and used by permission; and from *Why Am I Afraid to Tell You I'm a Christian?* by Don Posterski (Downers Grove, Ill.: InterVarsity Press, 1983); copyright © 1983 InterVarsity Christian Fellowship of the USA and used by permission.